"Daniel Felix passionately leads you through new ways that a great trustee epitomizes the virtue of loyalty. He teaches us the meaning of loyalty and how to discern what it requires of us in the extremely complex human relationship called a trust. His wisdom will carry you a long way toward achieving the high purpose of managing a trust." ~ James ("Jay") E. Hughes, Jr.

◆

"Daniel Felix's book, *The Way of the Trustee*, teaches the very basis of integrity itself, shining light on the elements that make people in tough jobs sink or swim. If you have been given the opportunity to stretch yourself in the job of Trustee, Dan's book is a must read." ~ Marguerite C. Lorenz, Executive Director, Lorenz Private Trustees

◆

"Beneficiaries need great trustees. Daniel Felix is a seasoned professional and shines a light on how trustees can be a force for good in the role. As a resource, *The Way of the Trustee* provides many great practices, tools, and thinking to help trustees fulfill their duty of loyalty, better serve beneficiaries, and navigate the ambiguities of what is a challenging role." ~ Lindsay Pope, Dean of the Trustscape, Purposeful Planning Institute

◆

"Being a Master Trustee is not a one-size-fits-all endeavor and one must be more than merely the gatekeeper of the checkbook. As Dan points out, meeting beneficiaries where they are (emotionally, intellectually, verbally) remains a key to successful outcomes. To do this, he offers the path to develop Trust Wisdom for enhancement of the life of the Beneficiary and the Trustee. And you will learn how to say yes and no for the right reasons." ~ Kevin Quinn, President, Independent Trustee Alliance

◆

"Dan has written a guide for trustees that is thoughtful, thought-provoking, wise, and practical. A book that should be read and reread not only by trustees, but by all who are touched by trusts." ~ Hartley Goldstone, Managing Director, Lineage Trust Company

◆

The Way of the Trustee

A Holistic Guide to Enlightened Trust Administration in Service to Families

Daniel P. Felix

Foreword by Peter White

James E. Hughes, Jr.
FOUNDATION
Publishing

This edition published in the United States of America by James E. Hughes, Jr. Publishing, 2000 Morris Avenue, Suite 1300, Birmingham, Alabama, 35203. James E. Hughes, Jr. Foundation Publishing is part of the James E. Hughes, Jr. Foundation. It furthers the mission of the Foundation to advance the field of family governance and generational well-being.

Cover design and book design/layout by Debra Kocis, Envision Impact, Inc. Editing services provided by Bonniejean Alford, Alford Enterprises. Photography by Barry Rustin Photography.

The moral rights of the author have been asserted.

The opinions expressed herein are those of the author and not any institution or person for which he might be affiliated.

Library of Congress Cataloging-in-Publication Data

Name:	Daniel P. Felix, author.
Title:	*The Way of the Trustee: A Holistic Guide to Enlightened Trust Administration in Service to Families*
Description:	James E. Hughes, Jr. Foundation Publishing
Identifiers:	ISBN 979-8-9886691-4-2 (hardcover)
	ISBN 979-8-9886691-7-3 (softcover)
	ISBN 979-8-9886691-8-0 (digital)

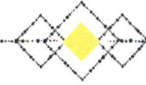

I
Dedicate
this book
to

my parents,
my children,

and

all those
family, friends, colleagues,
clients, and lovers

for showing me the way.

Daniel P. Felix

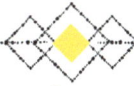

Table of Contents

Foreword

By Peter White

*D*an Felix is a gentle, good man, but he is also principled and direct. "The purpose of this book," he says in the opening sentence, "is to detail how the trustee can be a force of good for the family."

In the next paragraph he adds: "The question for me is whether [the] stakeholders are better off - in all ways and not just financially – by having a trust."

Traditionally, trusts have been used to control the beneficiaries' spending, protect the assets from scheming outsiders, and keep taxes as low as possible – all financial purposes. What then does Dan mean, "not just financially"?

A few years ago, I retired from a 30-year career helping individuals and families with what I called the experience of wealth. Focusing on experience differentiated my work because few people thought about wealth as a subjective phenomenon. We assumed that wealth was a good thing and weren't concerned about what it was like from the inside out. We had little time for the problems of wealthy people because we believed that if we had wealth, we would be happy, and so should they.

I was interested in the reality of wealth from the inside out. My approach was not about what to invest in or how to save on taxes, not how to prevent family members from squabbling, not even how to prevent inheritors from squandering. These were exterior issues. Experience is an interior perspective: not what is it? or how to control it? *But what does it feel like?* And what might make it feel better?

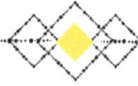

The important new question asked in *The Way of the Trustee* is, what does it feel like to be a "stakeholder" in family wealth held in trust? What's the experience like and what might a thoughtful trustee do to make it more rewarding?

And why not ask such a question? After all, the reason people leave wealth to others is so they will have better lives, right? Better lives happen from the inside out; they are defined by having better experience, not better stuff.

Dan is not inviting us to close our minds to the role of the trustee in financial issues, which is important, but to open them to the experience of wealth, which involves the struggle between abundance and meaning.

Contrary to what we often hear, money can make you happy.

Buy a new car. Spend a week in Paris. Have a hot fudge sundae. These work for me... Happy.

But the catch is – and this is big when it comes to the ideas and aspirations of many wealthy people – happiness, for all the good press it gets – it's even in the American Declaration of Independence – doesn't live up to its billing.

It doesn't last. It doesn't change you. It teaches you little or nothing. It doesn't help you learn who you are, why you exist, or what your life is about.

Many years and lots of ups and downs have shown me that life is about traversing a great arc from fear to love on a pathway of meaning. Fulfilling the promise of life is hard work and usually

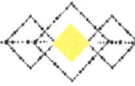

involves some suffering. With wealth you may be able to avoid painful struggle but in avoiding the struggle, you will probably miss the meaning.

The answers to the big questions of life come from plunging into the fray with the problems and opportunities life serves up to us, even the ones that make us unhappy. We can't imagine living without someone who dies. We're expelled from school. Our business is failing. We get arrested for DWI. The one we love betrays us.

These experiences, and the suffering they entail, are tough problems but with big money you can buy your way around them, whether it's paying someone else to solve them or taking on a nice big blob of happiness to make the feeling of suffering go away. This works for the moment, but you haven't grown because you haven't experienced and wrestled directly with the problem. You haven't taken the medicine life wanted you to have.

When you remain an adolescent as an adult you have trouble taking responsibility. You may have friends and admirers, but you aren't a friend to yourself. You have trouble enjoying things as they are; you're always planning; you're moving on to the next person, place or thing, the next new thing, the coming excitement – because the here and now aren't enough. With wealth blindly used, it is often and sadly true that nothing is enough because you aren't enough, and so long as your sights are fixed on happiness alone, you may never be.

Viktor Frankl's classic book *Man's Search for Meaning* is the story of his internment in a Nazi concentration camp during the

Holocaust. Frankl, who was a Jew and a practicing psychiatrist, observed that survival against the extreme privations of camp life depended on more than physical robustness. Those who were able to stay alive were more or less in the same physical condition as those who died, but something enabled them to carry on. What was it?

Frankl realized that the survivors were the ones who sacrificed portions of their food for others, or comforted the sick and dying, or were able to make a small joke in the face of the horror, or participated hopefully in communal activities: those who, despite their own suffering, were able to find a reason for living in helping alleviate the suffering of others, which is to say meaning. They lived because their daily lives meant something. Frankl concluded that the search for meaning was the essential path for human beings in all circumstances.

In my work, I found Frankl's poignant observations as true on the manicured lawns of abundance as in the concentration camp. Those who were having a good experience of wealth were not those addicted to happiness but were people whose lives in work, relationship, and spirit were intrinsically significant to them. They were doing the right thing in the right way; to put it in Biblical terms, they were loving God and loving their neighbors as themselves.

Some describe meaning as intrinsic significance; others call it love; some call it God. No matter, it refers to the qualitative value one finds in leading one's life according to the particular call that

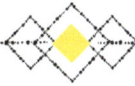

is there for everyone and the light that beckons us to rise above our worldly selves.

I have spoken about one of the problems of wealth that trustees can be concerned about – that of the beneficiary who uses wealth to avoid the troubling growth opportunities of life and so doesn't grow. But there are many others. Family dynamics can be extremely difficult in the context of wealth, where the younger generation may be encouraged to live out not their own dreams but those of their parents. Conflict is passed from one generation to the next unless it's resolved, and often it's not. Family is supposed to be a community of respect, care and fun – love, that is – but sometimes it ends up a field of disempowerment, contention, and despair.

Trusts themselves can be troubling because they can feel like the one who set up the trust for you doesn't trust you. Beneficiaries often feel like perpetual children to their trustee's perpetual parent. Trust grantors find themselves frustrated that money they have worked for since they were young men and women is now a source of conflict in the family instead of a source of fulfillment and family unity.

Trustees are right in the middle of all this, and the traditional function of the trustee is to exert control to solve problems or at least keep a lid on them. Trustees are often despised by the people they're trying to help because their one trick has been control. Use trust assets to make the people act differently or at least keep a lid on the problem, which usually isn't meaningful for any of the stakeholders.

The genius of Dan Felix's professional practice is his understanding that trustees are in a position to influence the experience of wealth for the better. A trustee can be a mentor, an adviser, a friend. The trustee can improve the quality of interactions among everyone in the trust stakeholding. The trustee can teach the beneficiaries as well as grantors. The trustee can learn as he or she goes on the journey with the stakeholders.

In short, and not to get too carried away, Dan is showing us how trustees can move from controlling those in the trust milieu to loving them in the broadest sense of the word.

The point is, the financial issues around trusts are not more important than the experiential ones, a reality well known and honored by my friend Dan Felix, who has plunged into the psychospiritual waters and shown everyone involved in the trust stakeholding how to swim toward the welcoming shore of meaning.

Author's Preface

I began the manuscript for this book almost ten years ago. Feeling a compulsion to describe the road in front of me, I devoted almost every Sunday for some nine months until a complete draft took shape.

This necessity provided an account for myself and for my budding trustee practice. To make a record. To connect the many dots – and in some cases, just to note the dots. To take it out of my head and to lay it out so I could see the wisdom of what was there – and to perhaps get insights as to what wasn't.

I also needed to lay out the map of what I and other like-minded practitioners held as appropriate trust administration. Inspired by the vision of Peter White, Jay Hughes, and others, I in turn, developed my own formula for generative trust administration. I felt the need to hoist my own flag, at least enough to serve as a salute to those that came before.

The above explains, among other things, the book's reference to the trustee as "he." That he is me, and not a narrowed view that trustees are all male.

Over time, a few things happened.

For one, my own journey as trustee has continued and expanded. New clients, different trusts and roles, wonderful successes, and deep opportunities for learning – some might even call them failures. I have been joined by others, both in the profession and in my firm. And from time to time, I took out the manuscript – and Peter's introduction – and devoured it, imprinting it more deeply into myself.

I would also assemble excerpts for teaching and seminars. At some point, I realized it would be better to have a tangible book to teach from and to share. Thus, I made the decision to create this book, despite a couple of issues.

First, this is not the book I would write today. Perhaps the biggest two changes: I would more deeply emphasize the wisdom to employ compassion – to self, to all others, and to the many crying wounds of the world. I would also say (even) more about effective communication and offer specific examples and possible approaches. Compassion and communication are interconnected and foundational to all successful relationships, especially those of a trustee.

All the same, I couldn't resist inserting a few updates into the text. I've tagged them as "Update."

Second, I don't know who needs or wants to take in what I am saying. Not having an audience in mind beyond myself in the writing, the journey of this book remains to be seen: Will it be helpful to a few who take on the role of trustee? I hope so. Beyond that? I don't know. We'll find out. And I am excited to see how it unfolds.

In the meantime, the thoughts needed to come out. And here they are.

" *The concept of duty, which seems dreary and burdensome, aligns individual and collective interest. Duty may frustrate impulse, but duty gives the edge over time to the one who is self-aware. Duty is prepared to sacrifice short-run desire to secure long-run meaning.*

~ Peter White, Ecology of Being

"

Introduction

> **"**
>
> *It is not incumbent upon you to complete the work, but neither are you at liberty to desist from it.*
>
> *~ Pirkei Avot*
>
> **"**

A trustee can be a force of good for the family. Unfortunately, many books about serving as a trustee focus instead on the legal minimums and select legal and financial technical considerations. No book that I'm aware of provides a roadmap for the trustee on how to think about and approach the trust so that the grantor, his beneficiary, and the family are better off.

The question for me is how these stakeholders are better off – in all ways, and not just financially – by having a trust. While on a journey, though it's good to watch out for potholes in the road; knowing why one is on the road at all remains more important. Accordingly, I focus on both the legal/financial component as well as the relational and spiritual components of this journey.

The context of trusts typically includes the fulfillment of both the individual and family not only in their present manifestation

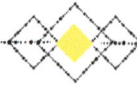

but simultaneously, knitted together in the fabric built over generations. To me, that's a holy tapestry.

While some believe that the trust document itself will dictate success or failure, they ignore other essential questions, particularly *how* the document will be administered and *what impact* that administration will have. Consider, as an example, our Constitution for the United States of America. While the document is essential in distinguishing what happens in this country, it is not self-executing. People are required to bring its intention into reality. In fact, the determining factor is *how* the document will be interpreted and applied. Further, *who* is serving in Washington, D.C. at any given time and *how* they are acting makes a difference in the lives of the people in the United States, if not the world.

So, too with a trust: *how* the trust is being administered, *what* is the administration's agenda and *who* is doing it – all make a critical difference. It is remarkable that there is a general misunderstanding of this difference, which for me stems from ignorance of both what a trustee does as well as the power of a trust.

In my more than thirty years serving as a trustee and in studying the practice, I am stunned by the power of a trust for both good and for disaster. On the one hand, trusts have been the vehicle to help families thrive over generations; while on the other, families have fragmented and squandered huge financial and human resources through the mishandling of their trusts. This is what's at stake in the administration of trusts.

By focusing on the trustee, I do not mean to minimize the critical importance of other stakeholders in determining the success or failure of a trust. A short list of the typical stakeholders includes other fiduciaries, trusted advisors, and especially, the family itself, from the creators of the trust to their descendants. Others have offered helpful advice for those audiences, those that I found helpful are referenced in the Bibliography along with sources for the content of the book. This book will help inform their thinking and actions on the subject as well.

This book aims to provide context and advance the discussion of *how* and *why* the trustee thinks and behaves. Hopefully, it will be a guide both in terms of the context of trust administration generally and some specific known phenomena.

One known issue relates to the misplaced reliance on the trust's language to the complete exclusion of the impact of the trust. Besides being philosophically and morally repugnant, such an approach fails to address reality. If this book could have but one result, I hope it will be to remove that damaging misconception. Accordingly, this book aims to be a proof-text for the idea that successful trust administration demands careful attention to the beneficiaries as well as to the trust creator, their wishes, and the trust documents.

Thank you for joining me on this journey. May you learn much and help build the holistic practice of trust administration.

Section One

Why a Trustee? Why a Trust?
Why this Book?

> " *To be human is a problem, and the problem expresses itself in anguish.*
>
> ~ **Abraham Joshua Heschel** "

The need for a trust reaches deep inside humankind. This need is an inescapable part of the human condition. Our earliest records document efforts to address this need on a number of levels. Over time, those methods to deal with this need have evolved into our current trust practices.

This history has evolved a vision of the different ways to envision the idealized trustee both as to the good and the bad. These visions manifest as archetypes of the trustee.

In this Section, I will outline these foundational pieces.

Chapter One
The Human Condition

An inescapable part of the human condition is that there are times when we need to rely on others to take care of us. We need others when we can't do it ourselves. There's a nice question as to whether we ever *can* or *should* be considered independent. Consider the implications of the poetical observation that no man is an island or in the observation of the genius Albert Einstein who reportedly stated that he experienced expanding amazement at how dependent we are on each other in society.

The first time we need help in our lives is as an infant. We are unable to take care of ourselves until many years after birth. There's a nice debate as to when, if ever, we are fully independent. Consider for example various legal recognitions: for driving a car, for voting, for serving in the military, for not attending school. Also compare the custom of *b'nai mitzvah* at age 13. Some Jewish communities clarify that this passage indicates the celebrant as being able to participate in Jewish activity *as a full member of the community*, or that the parents are no longer responsible for their offspring *as a child*.

Some also are dependent in our society given their special needs or circumstances arising from their birth, disease, or trauma. Our current label for this dependency is disability.

In addition to disability incurred at birth or through trauma, there is often a period of disability towards the end of a human life. Increasingly, the aging process seems to be accompanied by an expanded period of disability.

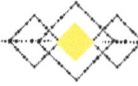

Finally, we also need the participation of others at our death in dealing with our corpse, our surviving family, and our other effects.

As a culture, we're clear on what this help looks like. We insist on respect of our dignity, our wishes, our needs, and our feelings. In fact, to the extent that we can articulate it, we believe that the helper should follow our exact directions on how we want to be helped.

In our present culture in the United States of America, personal choice is generally deferred to over considerations of the impact of that choice. In this author's lifetime, there has been a growing tendency to balance personal choice and impact – impact on both the individual as well as on others. Consider, for example, the limitations placed on the choice to smoke tobacco, which during my lifetime has run from smoking being rarely restricted to the opposite. This openness to the impact of the choice is not yet as apparent in the trustscape: trust and estate attorneys seem to rarely question or engage, let alone challenge a trust creator whose wishes may have all sorts of impact. This includes a trust creator's decision to disinherit one of his children. And yet, the impact of disinheritance can have a highly negative impact on the family's relationships and happiness, from alienation to lawsuits.

The need for this help is inescapable for individuals and their families, and so, on a larger scale, for our society. Where the support is provided well and is well received, not just the individuals and their families flourish but also society at large. And conversely, where the support is not provided or received well, all suffer.

The greater the number of families with an ill-fitting or mis-performing trustee, the worse for our society as well as for those

particular families. Currently, we are experiencing an epidemic of bad trust administration. There is a spike in the number of families suing each other over the administration of their estates[1] with presumably a greater number of families who simply break up, rather than file a lawsuit. This statistic suggests a significant tear in the social fabric.

I intend this book to help those who intend to reverse this trend, so that more families have a positive experience with their trusts. As individuals, as families, and as communities we need some effective means to deal with these situations.

I hope to add to the discussion of effective means to deal with these inescapable issues with this book. We can then sketch out pieces of our experience: our heritage and history, our attitudes and intentions, and our practices.

---

[1] As reported by the Honorable James G. Riley, Supervising Judge, Circuit Court of Cook County (the county including Chicago, my hometown), Probate Division in his panel discussion October 31, 2014, hosted by Advocate Charitable Foundation and Northern Trust.

Chapter Two
The Biblical Foundation

The Torah[2] contains some helpful insights as to the transitions of the founders of the Jewish tribe. While a deeper discussion of mourning practices is beyond the scope of this book, these practices are, nevertheless, important in the bigger picture of intergenerational transition, as well as in the wisdom offered in the Torah.

Paradoxically, the name of the chapter which begins with the death of Abraham's wife, Sarah, is called *The Life of Sarah*.[3] After grieving over the death of Sarah, Abraham negotiates the purchase of a cave in Hebron for her and his dead to be buried.

Great attention is given to his negotiation, and his paying the seller's expression of the price. This focus underscores the need for a secure burial ground. If the purchase isn't enough to create this security, the land is within the boundaries where what God will identify to Abraham's descendants as the Promised Land.

It's said that the first responsibility of a Jew who begins to reside in a new location is to make sure there is a suitable place to be buried. This is truly an example of the practice of beginning with the end in mind.

Abraham gave all that he owned to Isaac and gave gifts while living to his other sons. He is not reported to have blessed any of his descendants at the end of his life. Nevertheless, Abraham blessed

---

2 The choice of the Torah reflects my personal culture. I welcome an analysis from the perspectives of other religions and wisdom traditions, especially as to how they would advance the discussion of intergenerational transition generally and *the Way of the Trustee* specifically. For a deeper treatment of the subject from a Jewish perspective, see for example, "Living and Dying in Ancient Times: Death, Burial, and Mourning in Biblical Tradition" by Simcha Paull Raphael, Albion-Andalus, 2015.

3 Specifically, "*Chaye Sarah*." Genesis 23. All references here are to *Torah: A Modern Commentary*, edited by W. Gunther Plaut, 1981, Union of American Hebrew Congregations.

Ishmael at his birth, and God himself is said to have blessed Isaac after Abraham's death.

Abraham's two sons, Isaac and Ishmael, come together to bury him in the cave at Hebron. There is no discussion of how they chose the same cave; perhaps that was the presumption. Abraham's negotiation for the cave's purchase following the death of Sarah did not include mention of himself, other than for him to be able to bury his dead there. Could Abraham not expressly contemplate or mention his own mortality?

Abraham's two sons coming together to bury him is more remarkable because there's no evidence that the sons were close or in any ongoing relationship. What's more, the Torah does not report that either son spoke with their father proximate to death. Specifically, Isaac is not reported to have spoken to his father after his father bound him for sacrifice many years before. Similarly, Ishmael was separated as an infant when his father took Sarah's request for banishment of his mother, Hagar, as his action plan.

One explanation for the coming together of Isaac and Ishmael may have been an implicit cultural imperative: children, however estranged, get together to bury their parent. It was just something that was done. Another possibility is aspirational: this coming together is something that was hoped for.

It also appears that none of Abraham's descendants by his second wife participated in his burial. His second wife was not mentioned in the text as being buried in the cave, and his servant and mother of his son Ishmael, Hagar, was not either.

Later, Isaac, prematurely perceiving the imminent end of his life, gives his special blessing to his younger son, Jacob, instead of to

the older Esau. This gift engineered in part with Rebecca, Isaac's wife, violated Isaac's wishes, including to comply with the custom to give to the eldest male. Isaac does bestow a lesser blessing on Esau, who expresses a murderous intention towards Jacob. And so, Jacob flees the family.

Much attention is given to the reuniting of these two years later from the point of view of Jacob's anxiety that Esau will punish him for conspiring to deprive Esau of his birthright blessing. The significance of the reunification is highlighted by Jacob's wrestling with the angel the night before. The angel bestows Jacob with a new name, Israel, meaning one who wrestles with beings divine and human.

Much to Jacob's relief, the reunification is quite positive, flowing perhaps in part from the abundance that Esau obtained without his father's last blessing, and perhaps also because of the gifts Jacob offers Esau as part of his anxiety-inspired precautions. Given Esau's hospitality to Jacob, we can also speculate on the enlightenment of Esau contributing to the positive reunion as well.

When the end of his days does approach many years later, Isaac is conveniently relocated in Hebron ready to be buried with his father in the cave. His two sons, Esau and Jacob, already reunited, come together and cooperate in their father's burial, like their forebears, Isaac and Ishmael.

And so, the coming together of Jacob and Esau is given explanation. However much this was the hoped-for practice, their reunification is credited at least in part with some planned action by Jacob.

And there appears to be a continuing difference in that ancient telling in how women are treated. There's no discussion in the text of what provisions Isaac made for his surviving wife, Rebecca, although Jacob claims that she was buried in the Hebron cave, where he claims to have buried his wife, Leah. Perhaps feeling the need for completion, there is discussion outside the text that Rebecca was buried with her husband in the Hebron cave.

In his turn, at the end of his life, Jacob requests Joseph bury him in the family cave. In anticipation of his death, Jacob gives a double portion and positive blessings to Joseph, who is one of his youngest sons, and to Joseph's two sons, particularly the younger, Ephriam. In these blessings, Jacob again undermines the favoring of the first born in the transfer of certain gifts from the prior generation. Contrary to Jacob's example, orthodox Jewish practice continues to favor the first-born male.

To all his sons, Jacob offers his vision of what will happen to each of them. In poetic format, these final words include blessings and curses as well as aspirations, assessments, warnings, and recollections. There appears no record of how Jacob's other sons received any of these final words.

Jacob then repeats his burial instructions to all his sons. This could be a reflection of Jacob's proven penchant for planning or deference to his hard-learned insight to include all his sons in his favor, and not just Joseph.

With Jacob's death, Joseph's brothers fear for Joseph's revenge against them for having sold him into slavery. They tell Joseph of their father's deathbed request for the powerful Joseph to treat them well. Their communication contains both explicit and

implicit begging for Joseph's forgiveness. This fear is resonant of the heightened emotionality over perceived past familial injustices common to the loss of a family member.

Joseph is brought to tears by the request, and kindly reassures them that though the brothers may have intended him harm, God intended their actions for the good. And so, Joseph manifests a wise and merciful course of conduct from looking at a bigger perspective, that is, from God's point of view.

As with Isaac, there's no report of how Jacob's surviving wives were to be treated or what portion, if any, was to be theirs.

Joseph, following the practice in Egypt, where he long lived and had adopted various customs, has Jacob's body embalmed. And so, we are connected for the first time with this post-death practice.

With the approval of Pharaoh, Joseph and his brothers journey to the land of Canaan to bury their father back in the cave in Hebron.

Later, anticipating his own approaching death, Joseph makes his burial request to his brothers. Specifically, he requests he be buried in the Promised Land. His body is not only embalmed but is placed in a coffin, the first reference to this device.

Unspoken is the power of Joseph's vision of a promised land and request, and the potential for both the curse of being a burden and the blessing of the inspiration in this extremely long funeral procession.[4]

Many generations after Joseph's death, Moses, not a direct descendant, though the leader of the tribe, assumes responsibility for carrying

---

4 Characterizing the Sinai journey as part funeral procession comes from Simcha Raphael, Da'at Institute. For his fascinating article about this and other significant, but rarely examined parts of the Joseph story, see http://www.daatinstitute.net/wp-content/uploads/2013/04/JosephsBonesDAAT.pdf

the bones of Joseph.[5] Though God takes Moses' life before he enters Israel, the tribe does have Joseph's bones interred there.[6]

Among other things, these stories show the basic need for dealing with last messages (blessings and curses) as well as the due disposition of the corpse. All are afforded a timely opportunity to make their end of life wishes known. Joseph accelerates the process addressing the subject of his death at the time of death of his father, not waiting until the cusp of his own death.

The focus is on the articulation and enforcement of the individual's needs and wishes. His family and community are expected to honor those wishes. Those individual wishes are also engaged in a dance with custom and tradition.

The evidence favoring the individual over tradition is evidenced twice by Jacob in the custom of the birthright blessing belonging to the first-born. First, as a recipient of this blessing from his father, Jacob bypasses his older brother. Then later, Jacob again bypasses the oldest male, when he extends the first-born's blessing to Joseph's second born.

Another feature favoring custom and tradition is the coming together of hostile or at least estranged family members for burial of the preceding generation–first, Isaac and Ishmael and then Jacob and Esau.

---

5 Exodus 13:19. *Torah: A Modern Commentary,* edited by W. Gunther Plaut, 1981, Union of American Hebrew Congregations.

6 Joshua 24:32. *Torah: A Modern Commentary,* edited by W. Gunther Plaut, 1981, Union of American Hebrew Congregations.

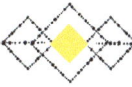

The *impact* of the individual's choices – including of the curses to the survivors – becomes express in a few small, though significant ways. We receive some insights in three instances:

- *On the impact on both Esau and Jacob of Isaac's misplaced blessing,*

- *From Joseph's attempt to redirect Jacob's blessing of Joseph's sons, and*

- *The invention of protection in Jacob's deathbed statements by Joseph's brothers.*

Note that individual choice is specifically the choice of males and not females. Further, this emphasis on the right to choose evidences a preference towards masculine energy, as much as the disregard of the impact of their decisions on the rest of their family. Although explainable by the male-dominated culture of the time, it also demonstrates masculine's shadow side and a failure to appreciate and incorporate needed feminine energy.

There's also very little expressly of God's hand in these portions of the Torah. Arguably this generational transition is in the context of establishing God's vision, such as God's promise to prosper Abraham's family like grains of sand in the desert. The advantages offered by a bigger perspective is suggested by Joseph's application of this big mind in his wise and calm reassurance to his brothers that he would continue to treat them well, even after the death of Jacob, their father.

The ideas, relationships and energies embedded in these biblical stories continue to resonate.

Chapter Three
Historical Antecedents

The legalistic structure of a trust arose out of the confluence of English law with historical necessity. While a detailed history of trusts is beyond the scope of this book, it may be helpful to note a couple of highlights.

The distinctions of English law separated the *idea* of ownership with the *benefits* of ownership. The trustee technically owns the assets of the trust. He's the only one who can direct the disposition of a trust asset. So, for example, his signature is required on checks. However, the trustee cannot use the trust assets for his own benefit; instead, he may use them only on behalf of those identified as the trust's beneficiaries.

The historical necessity was the waging of war, specifically English nobles leaving their families and realms to fight in the crusades. Trusts permitted an essential structure. These soldiers left their precious goods temporarily in the hands of the trustee, who would continue indefinitely in that role should the soldier never return.

Trusts were given life in the United States particularly in the whaling communities, where captains embarked on risky voyages, left their families and other assets in the hands of a trustee, who was typically already serving as their attorney.

How any of the resulting trusts fared under these trustees is not readily available to me and not the point of this book.

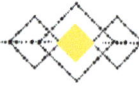

Note again the masculine – not just male – orientation of the context: wars and hunting, and a stewardship of possessions, including wife and family.

Alexander Hamilton is credited with helping to move the trust format forward in creating a trust structure with ongoing trustees to provide the deathbed wish of a sea captain to care for retired sailors. Hamilton's ingenuity was to assign trustee responsibilities to a committee which was staffed via title. Specifically, the trustee committee consisted of various elected officials, including The Mayor of New York City, and various ministers of several denominations.

Hamilton's ingenuity allowed for trust administration that could smoothly continue following the unavailability of any particular trustee. As a pattern for dealing with more routine family situations, his idea was not fully appreciated until almost a century later, when in the 1890s the use of trusts is said to have become common practice.

Chapter Four
Current Practices

*G*iven these antecedents it shouldn't be surprising that trusts are the preferred structure to accomplish intergenerational transition and continue to resonate in the masculine.

Trusts provide a legal structure which helps make ownership clear, based on the directions of the trust creator. Trusts are a mechanism to avoid court, namely, probate proceedings. They also provide a mechanism for tax planning.

Among the alternatives, they maximize the trust creator's control and influence. Alternatives include joint ownership, or even gifting. These alternatives put the assets at risk not only of the co-owner's discretion, but also his creditors.

The fact is that trusts are embedded into our reality. And it may be that however flawed, they are the best structure currently available.

One of the significant flaws of trusts is that, outside of the discussion in some families of significant wealth, there is scant attention to how trusts may be used to enhance or empower the family or how they may be used to enhance an individual's non-financial assets, such as a family's values or legacy.

One inspired approach looks to trusts along with other structures to protect against the collapse of a family business in three

generations.[7] This entropy is a known phenomenon, popularly referred to as "shirtsleeves to shirtsleeves in three generations."

A stable and abundant economic foundation is certainly a blessing for a family.

Further, the practices supporting that blessing can provide additional benefits for a family in deepening relationships, honoring the elderly, and resolving conflicts, among others. And many of these practices are scalable to families of modest financial resources.

Curiously, there seems to be little discussion addressing what factors make a trust – or a particular trust administration – successful.[8] Is it simply by making the transition of legal ownership? Or is it helping the family thrive?

There is a need to define and construct a successful trust. *In this book, I offer a vision of successful trust administration which asks: how much better off is the family because of the trust?* This is not necessarily a financial measure. The trust's funds can be invested in education or other personal growth. Rather, the criteria span the whole of individual and family fulfillment.

---

7 See, for example and particularly, *Family Wealth, Keeping it in the Family: How Family Members and Their Advisors Preserve Human, Intellectual and Financial Assets for Generations*, by James E. Hughes, Jr., 2004, Bloomberg Press. Hughes has been a terrific advocate for creating structures and cultures which support families, especially to delay the inevitable loss of their financial fortune.

8 In addition to Hughes, the strong voice for purposeful trust administration can be heard in the voices of Hartley Goldstone and John A. Warnick.

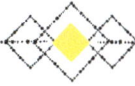

Chapter Five
Archetypes for the Trustee

L ooking briefly at a few models of trustees, both the good trustee as well as the bad one, can provide a shortcut for our vision.

The archetype of the successful trustee has been described as *philosopher king*. The term philosopher is used to express wisdom, while the word king embodies a person who acts and orders others for the benefit of his realm. In this case, the realm being the trust.

There is little in the literature about how an inspired trustee may develop towards becoming a philosopher king. This book aspires to provide direction on that development. In the book, I identify best practices and tools of mastery. This book is NOT about minimum practices, but about best practices and how an aspiring trustee may be of deeper help to the families he serves.

The development of trust law allows for structural support for the philosopher king trustee. Trust protectors, advisory committees, and the like can provide helpful checks and balances. These supports may have been brought in because of the absence of philosopher king candidates, or perhaps better, because however wise the trustee, they will function better with this help.

I submit that we should aspire to this archetype, even though we know we will execute imperfectly. Our imperfection need not be an obstacle to enlightened administration.

The trustee's role as a temporary substitute leader for the family calls on the archetype of *regent*. This archetype resonates especially

where the trustee is serving temporarily, such as, for a younger person who does not receive the trust assets until he becomes older.

Sometimes a king must do battle, especially to protect his realm. This is called the archetype of the *warrior*. I will say more about this essential role of trustee, especially as protector, as noted later within the book.

The archetypes we've looked at so far are all based in masculine energy. In fact, it is necessary to expressly state that the trustee is often serving as a *father figure*, and often carries the energy of the father who was the creator of the wealth, if not also of the trust.

These archetypes demonstrate that masculine energy is essential. Simultaneously, I submit that truly successful trust administration benefits from due embodiment of feminine energy. This feminine can manifest as acceptance for people as they are, as joy in the creative aspects of a family's culture, and in a nurturing approach, among others. This feminine energy invokes the models of *mother* and *queen*.

The masterful trustee would do well to also consider the archetype of *servant leader* and the closely related model of *personne de confiance*. Servant leadership requires the leader to be first a servant and to look to whether the other's needs are being met. Similarly, the *personne de confiance* is the reliable advisor to the king.

These models strongly embody the quality of loyalty. I contend that loyalty is the key attribute of a trustee and will talk more about it.

Though there are few historical examples of females serving as *personne de confiance,* the supporting energy is feminine. In fact, not giving due attention to this more feminine role may be what causes so many lawyers to fail when they attempt to serve as trustee. As lawyers, they are more oriented toward the masculine and the warrior hero.

Models sharing both genders include the archetypes of *wizard, elder,* and *crone.* The best example of this may be Merlin, whose magical teaching of the young King Arthur empowers Arthur to greatness. A trustee's magic is his continued learning in various skills. I suggest skills in this book which might be considered for mastering successful trust administration.

It's worth our time to mention the shadow sides of some of these archetypes.

The *Tyrant King* and *Evil Queen* are cruel, overly demanding, abusive, and unsympathetic. Either gender can occupy this dark throne. I've seen this repeatedly in my own practice in the situation of the older brother, who because of material success, is named as trustee by his parents for his younger, and less financially successful brother. In these cases, the older brother becomes abusive and punitive in his communications and his handling of distributions.

Evil Stepparents are even worse, because they involve a more personal betrayal. Either a betrayal of the natural parent in associating with the evil stepparent which leads to the abandonment (or worse) of his child, or on the part of the stepparent who appears at first to be good, but later is revealed as evil. Let's take as example the well-known case of *Spencer v. DiCola*. The family may have identified the trustee, whom they sued, in this way as an evil stepparent. That family had actually selected and hired this trustee only a few years before they sued her. In this context, one can imagine that the family found the trustee to be not what they thought, and that her denial of their distribution requests constituted a betrayal of their consideration in hiring her originally. I'll come back to this case at various points in the book.

On the other hand, the shadow archetypes of the *Absent King* or the *Ice Queen* are characterized by indifference and non-responsiveness. I've seen this manifested by a few trustees in their unreasonable delays in responding to requests or even in performing basic administrative tasks. Consistent with the archetype, those trustees offered no advance notice of their delay, and no meaningful apology after.

Archetypes also help sketch out the story of a trust's administration. Afterall, one can quickly gather the difference of a trust administered by a philosopher king as opposed to one administered by an evil king. In fact, even outsiders, ultimately

including a judge being called upon to resolve a dispute over the trust, may well be influenced by the perception of what archetype best fits the trustee.

The story, in turn, can provide a context for actions for a trust's stakeholders. Helping the stakeholders understand how a certain decision is consistent with ongoing generative administration may help avoid unrest. Further, in addition to the impact on the trust's stakeholders, a trustee's deliberate choice of their archetype can help them develop towards that ideal.

With this background, let us consider in more detail the practices and perspectives, which form the ideal playbook for the trustee.

Section Two
Practices and Perspectives
of the Trustee

> *Practice isn't the thing you do once you're good.*
> *It's the thing you do that makes you good.*
>
> ~ *Malcolm Gladwell*

I submit that the organizing consideration is the virtue of loyalty, for which I identify key practices of the trustee. First, the six core practices of the trustee, and then a dozen other supportive practices. Finally, we'll identify and describe some advanced tools for a master trustee, which assist in the trustee's mindset and practice.

We'll devote special attention in this part to polarity thinking, which is a specialized approach to the interdependencies inherent in the trustscape. Hartley Goldstone is credited with inventing the term "trustscape" to define the entire system of family and others connected by the trust, including, but not limited to,

the trustee, the trust creator or grantor, the beneficiary, or the trusted advisors.[9]

It could be most effective and accurate to describe the progress of a trustee's learning as a journey to mastery. Though mistakes and other sources of learning will continue, mastery is a time-tested, even if somewhat imprecise measure of a level of competence that supports an independent practice. The path from the newcomer past the apprentice level is evidenced by the alternative name for a master, namely journeyman. And the journey is a wonderful model utilized through history and literature in various cultures.

A trustee who is committed to the journey of mastery may well consider three overlapping, synergistic perspectives: kavanah (intention), polarity thinking (key guidance for a trust's interdependencies), and the five energies (the multi-dimensionality of reality).

My goal in this section is to bring the reader's attention to the usefulness and importance of these practices and perspectives, leaving the reader to further study each one as you may find fit.

9 Specifically, Hartley defined the trustscape as "a subsystem within the larger family system. Members of the trustscape are those connected by a trust agreement – trust-creators, trustees, beneficiaries, trust-protectors, committees, and their advisors."

Chapter Six
Loyalty

W e may have pictures in our head of the loyal friend or the loyal pet. What are the attributes? Don't they have a certain steadfastness of service, and of being there for you? Of attentiveness: acting and being as if there is no other place to be than by your side? There is also the attribute of nonjudgmental, if not also sympathetic and empathetic listening. Loyalty is also equated with fidelity.[10]

From a more thoughtful source: the American philosopher Josiah Royce defined loyalty compellingly in his 1908 collection of his essays on the Philosophy of Loyalty as "the willing and practical and thoroughgoing devotion of a person to a cause."

Unpacking this definition, notice that his use of the word devotion does bring greater clarity. Devotion brings in the element of a beloved, as we speak of a spouse being devoted to her significant other, or a parent being devoted to a child. The word devotion also has an important spiritual aspect, being used religiously.

Royce's descriptors of being "willing, practical, and thoroughgoing" are also helpful. First, there's help in the idea of devotion being willing, that is voluntary and intentional. The trustee being willing to step up to the job of serving as trustee is important. Willingness also implies an invitation or calling. Dabbling at being a trustee or treating

---

10 Loyalty is probably the better term, given that it is a term used in defining the legal duties of a trustee and so already a part of trustscape vocabulary. Distracting associations for the word fidelity arise from the eponymous investment company as well as by the United States Marines.

it as a mere business or part-time volunteer position are limitations on being fully willing.

The idea of being practical adds a physical energy that is real and helpful to the trustee's job. Ungrounded abstract legalism is not practical. Focus on family empowerment at the expense of financial stability is not practical – nor is the reverse. The idea of practicality engages the concept and value of prudence.

The last term, thoroughgoing, is not in common use today. It means attending to every detail. I would add that this means attending to every *valence* as well. For one example: the loyal trustee understands that family financials operate largely on the emotional level.

These additional attributes of loyalty – willing, practical, and thoroughgoing – are all helpful in adding meaning to the concept of a fiduciary relationship, a special type of the legal relationship of principal and agent.

Loyalty in Relationship.

Royce's definition lends further guidance where he reminds us that loyalty exists in relationships, that loyalty is something that's done *to* something or someone else. This reminds us that loyalty cannot exist as a mere intention only, but that it must be manifested *for* something or someone. It's a *relationship*.

And this can be a relationship to Self. In being loyal to an ideal, for example, a code of conduct, one can be accurately said to be loyal to oneself, or sense of Self. I prefer to distinguish "Self" from "self" – Self with capital "S" being authentic, aligned with God and the universe, as opposed to loyalty to small "s" self – as in self-serving, ego-driven, within the mask.

It can even be said that loyalty to the ideal and the practice of loyalty makes available an even deeper loyalty to the family a trustee serves.

Morality and Loyalty.

Much of the commentary of Royce focuses on the moral component of loyalty. Can it truly be said that one can be loyal to an immoral cause. In other words, is the term "loyal Nazi" a contradiction in terms? More to our world, what is the prudent course if one were Hitler's trustee? Or more commonly, what is the prudent course of the trustee where a key stakeholder is engaged in some crime or immorality or not empowering practice? This can be a most difficult situation.

In dealing with morality, it can be important as to how the trustee assesses his own power and ability to influence the applicable stakeholders back to moral ground. Too often actors don't have an accurate grasp of their influence – sometimes both under and over-estimating their impact. Feedback from a wise, impartial coach or mentor can be helpful.

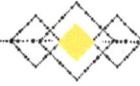

Loyalty and the Law.

The law is essential as a minimum standard and so is appropriate as one of the starting places. There can be a certain level of plasticity of the law, given the options in many jurisdictions to revise various trust provisions, often even without the approval of the court. Reasonable people may disagree on how the existing terms and possible revisions interplay with the loyalty due to the trust's stakeholders.

Too often trust stakeholders also end their considerations of loyalty with the provisions of the law. The best practice approach is often ahead of the minimum boundaries set by the law. That's because we are looking at the fullest expression of fiduciary care not limited by law. I discuss more on the law's benefits and limitations further along in the book.

A Trustee's Dual Loyalty.

I tweak Royce's definition to suggest that *the loyalty to be exercised by the family trustee is a willing and practical and thoroughgoing devotion to the trust creator and to the beneficiaries.* This devotion lives in the context of trust administration, that is, not only in the context of the legal (the law and the documents) and the assets, but also in the culture of the stakeholders.

Necessarily how that devotion manifests to the trust creator is different than that for the beneficiaries. The devotion due the trust

creator is to manifest his vision and to take care of the objects of his affection, when he himself is not there to attend to them sufficiently. Simply, it is to help the trust creator make his gift. Others, particularly Hughes, have developed this concept of the trust as a gift between generations..

On the other hand, the devotion due to the beneficiaries is to help them to receive this gift from the trust creator and to integrate it into a positive. This is what is meant by defining *the trustee's ultimate purpose or telos as "honoring the trust creator and empowering the beneficiaries."*

The qualifying phrase "in the context of trust administration" necessarily distinguishes the activities of a trustee from any of those many others who may be called to serve families. Further, trust administration itself is not only the platform of the trustee's services, but it is also his profession. Recognizing this is also necessary to acknowledge the duties and boundaries imposed on the trustee by his profession, and the reciprocal influence a trustee has upon his profession. So, again, the trustee has a duty of loyalty to his profession.

A great family trustee may also use his discretion to consider the family as a whole: the gifts from prior generations as well as how future generations may receive what is now on the table.

Update: Treatises could be written on the various duties that flow from a trustee's Duty of Loyalty. Colleagues Lindsay Pope and Frank Mullins are currently giving a trustee's Duty to Exercise Care some special attention. They're moving beyond minimum duties into best practices, particularly investigating how a generative trustee can develop a Culture of Care that enhances the flourishing of trust beneficiaries. There are many important questions being raised by this innovative approach. Near the top may be whether the trustee has discretion to invest additional time into building a substantive relationship with the beneficiary in order to make more mindful and life-enhancing distributions.

Chapter Seven
The Six Core Practices of the Trustee

To be loyal and effective as a trustee, I suggest a trustee do these six things:

- Establish "What Is"
- DO What's Best
- Protect "What Is"
- Communicate
- Build Trust
- Foster growth

I identify these six core practices here and consider them more deeply as part of the trustee's Playbook in Section Five. For now, I offer concise explanations.

Find Out What Needs to be Done and Do It.

Put another way: exercise both investigative awareness and willingness to act as explanation for a combined application of core practices one and two.

Devotion requires a recognition of what is going on and what should be done about it. A good dog's ability to sense a child's sadness and to offer himself for petting is a simple, intuitive, and powerful example of these two practices in action.

Of course, many issues are not that simple or obvious – either in discovery or in deciding what to do.

Be a Protector.

Perhaps a subset of awareness and action, protectiveness is an attribute so emotionally distinctive and functionally important as to deserve separate mention. This is demonstrated by the parent providing appropriate protection for his child, whether from life-threatening hazards or from an unfortunate referee call on the athletic field or even from the child's internal demons.

Through his deep involvement in protecting the financial assets, the trustee has a protective responsibility for the other family assets as well – human, social, spiritual, and intellectual. It's even said, perhaps originally by Jay Hughes, that the trustee is the keeper of the dreams of the family. It's hard to imagine a more essential guard.

It's a highly moral role – one that often is mentioned as the trustee's moral code or moral imagination, or simply as stewardship.

Communicate.

Again, a subset of practical action, communication is essential, and often overlooked. The textbook example is the lawyer who is doing profoundly important work for the client, but because he doesn't make the time to communicate with his client, the client necessarily assumes the worst.

Given that the act of communication also serves to build trust and respect, as well as inspirational values, such as compassion

and love, the trustee who is better at employing communication skills may be rightfully considered more loyal.

Build Trust.

At a minimum, the trustee should be trustworthy, and employ practices to build trust over inevitable challenges to that trust. The first level in being trustworthy is for the trustee to be free of conflicts and distractions. Conflicts and distractions divert the trustee from his loyalty. Even the mere appearance of a conflict or distraction can reasonably raise questions as to the basis for the trustee's actions. When that happens, the power of a trustee is diminished or dissolved. *If a trustee is involved in the trust for other reasons than the telos, then he is not truly devoted.* As another example, if a father is attending an athletic game primarily to network with the other parents, wouldn't we be justified in challenging his loyalty to his child?

The conflicts of a trustee include those that are not waivable, and those that may, under certain circumstances with informed consent, be waived. Consider again that even the mere appearance of impropriety amounts to a threat against trust and confidence, and so should be avoided as a rule of best practices.

Ideally, the trustee builds a trusted relationship for himself with the various stakeholders, and also enhances the trust within the family and also with the trusted advisors.

Grow.

This admonition applies to both the trustee himself and to support growth in others. How devoted can the trustee be if he is not well suited or prepared to execute the devotion that is called upon him to provide?

Wouldn't we agree that the parent who learns the rules and strategies of a sports game, and appropriately shares them with his child would be more devoted than one who didn't? Similarly, a trustee who is able to listen without being distracted by his own emotions, and who is able to support the beneficiary wherever he may be in psycho/spiritual/intellectual development may be said to be more devoted than an equally talented trustee who does not have those internal capabilities.

These six core practices flowing from the loyalty of a trustee are worthy of closer scrutiny and are discussed in Section five of this book. Let's continue deeper into our discussion of Loyalty, specifically to acknowledge some of the other significant tools, skills, and mindsets for a trustee that flow from the virtue of loyalty.

Chapter Eight
A Dozen Additional Practices of the Trustee

My premise is that by applying the virtue of loyalty we may reveal much if not the entire range of the skills, tools, attributes, and mindset of the trustee. They're also exposed by thinking more deeply about the aforementioned six core practices of the trustee's playbook, which all flow from loyalty as well.

I've found it useful in my journey to develop a dozen other major practices, which I list here – and will refer to at various points. They stem both from loyalty and the six core practices.

Commit to Excellence.

To be loyal, one performs their service well. Can one be truly loyal who does not aspire to doing his best as well as to improvement? Given that few, if any, are born with expertise in the six core practices, it is the commitment to excellence which moves the trustee forward.

Excellence should be distinguished from perfection, which is impossible, and ultimately a destructive pursuit. Note also that the pursuit of excellence includes appropriately handling what will inevitably go wrong.

Cultivate Technical Knowledge.

One can fairly say that knowledge of certain technicalities of trusts include the legal and financial. This technical knowledge can be

helpful, even where such technical expertise is already available through other trusted advisors. Further, a trustee may serve better where he cultivates knowledge of those specific technical issues which may be unique to the trust or to some of the stakeholders at hand. For example, if a beneficiary is interested in a specific vocational or other passion, the trustee would be acting loyally by cultivating some knowledge of it. This necessarily aids in the six core practices.

The practice of cultivating technical knowledge also includes, and perhaps more critically to the trustee's success, the art and science around influence, around individual personality, and learning types and assessments, as well as family dynamics and family systems. I will discuss some important if less well-known areas of knowledge in the latter half of this Section. These include specifically, *kavanah*, Polarity Thinking, and the Five Energies.

Cultivate Intelligences.

Again, flowing from the idea that a trustee is practicing loyalty by cultivating his ability to better serve, the trustee should engage in cultivating his various intelligences, which include emotional and human intelligences as well as the intellectual. See specifically the tool of the five energies in chapter eleven for a related discussion.

Cultivate Being Wholly Present and Mindful.

Also known as spiritual intelligence, being present and mindful is key to developing a robust awareness. Awareness is key to establishing what is, as well as the other core practices.

This practice also includes an appropriate perspective for the journeys of all the trust participants, including his own. Such a perspective includes due consideration for risk of all involved, but not a hyperfocus on risk.

Be Meticulous.

As a necessary part of the core practices, the trustee must be capable with details. This is to know details (or to have them available), as well as to act on a detailed level. The former may include, for example, the pertinent financial numbers for the trust. The latter includes the fine steps of administration necessary for things to happen.

Being meticulous would particularly include consideration of each of the stakeholders of the trust. It's been recommended, for example, that a trustee on the path of excellence should think of his beneficiaries every day.[11]

---

11 I've heard this attributed to Jay Hughes, but am not aware of that advice appearing expressly in his writings.

Consider the Big Picture.

Simultaneous with being on top of the details, the trustee should know the big picture. In addition to the daily or monthly budget, the trustee should know how the trust spends over the span of the trust, such as, when the trust funds might be exhausted.

The big picture includes the trend of the beneficiary's life and learning and the interplay with the rest of the family. Also, the trustee may find it appropriate to consider the family in the context of its generations – such as Seventh generation thinking.[12] The big picture necessarily includes a conception of the spiritual.

Deliver Results.

The trustee is typically responsible for various deliverables, which may be established in the trust document or cocreated by him as part of his administration.

It's easy for all the stakeholders to hyperfocus on results, especially given the typical under-appreciation of the trustee's tasks by the other stakeholders. Helpful amelioration can come in part from the recognition that this practice is necessarily in dynamic tension with others, particularly the next.

---

12 This is the philosophy of considering seven generations into the future for sustainability of practice. It is rooted in Iroquois principles.

Honor Process.

So much of the trustee's success can hinge on how he engages the stakeholders in decision-making and communications. This practice flows from and supports every one of the six core practices.

Even at a minimum compliance level, a court first looks at what process the trustee followed to reach a given result. Again, honoring process does not mean that a trustee may ignore the results.

Be Honest and Transparent.

Being honest and transparent is essential to building trust, but it is not enough. In fact, it happens that without consideration of prudence and discretion, trust can be dissipated, if not destroyed.

Delivering transparency also mitigates against legal minimums. For example, while the legal requirement for a trustee may be to provide an accounting once a year, due consideration of family circumstances may lead the trustee to provide ongoing access to financial reports.

Exercise Prudence and Discretion.

A trustee must maintain the confidences of his clients and the trust. A trustee is also part diplomat, enjoying private information that he may reshape without distorting and present at an opportune time.

This practice is necessarily in dynamic tension with the practice of honesty and transparency, and at its best works creatively with his practice of building trust and growth.

Be Responsive and Available.

Be there, where you have to be. This includes availability, presence, and continuity. The classic loyalty trap of some parents is showing up as more devoted to their own after-hours work demands than to their child's sports games. Being there becomes an issue for trustees as to their accessibility, the presence that they bring when they are present, as well as the ongoing continuity which they provide.

I've heard many complaints about the nonresponsiveness of trustees. Other trustee complaints might have been bypassed by good communications. Efficiency and the need to move forward are often unfairly blamed for nonresponsiveness in the rejoinder, "I don't have time." True to the extent that this practice is necessarily in dynamic tension with others, particularly the next.

Set Boundaries and Limits.

This is also known as cultivate efficiency. Like a ship's captain, the trustee has to make sure that the ship gets to its destination, and everyone has as good a cruise as possible. This ultimate project management role particularly demands not getting stuck or sidelined.

It may be helpful to recall that the trustee cannot be all things to all people. Ultimately, he has to take responsibility to stand for one position to move the trust forward. He also has to be responsible for the amount of resources – time and money – which are to be appropriately devoted to a situation.

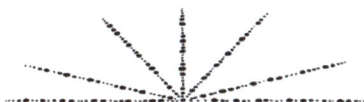

From this expansive immersion into the cause, one can understand Royce's argument that from loyalty all virtues flow.

Chapter Nine
Kavanah

Achieving mastery as a trustee requires the exploration into the consciousness of the trustee. This begins with a look at one's level of kavanah, pronounced "kah-vah-NAH" and means intention. From its root usage inside Jewish wisdom, it expresses a holy or holistic intention. This is to say, the trustee's intention and consciousness matters. It seeks to get to the spirit of the practice of being a trustee.

One aspect of this intention is the utilization of an I-Thou relationship, as articulated by Martin Buber. A human bond in a joint search for meaning and connection characterizes the I-Thou relationship. It is distinguished from an I-It relationship, which is impersonal, where one treats the other as an object. Too often a frustrated trustee falls into an I-It relationship, for example, with a so-called trust baby.

Spiral Dynamics.

The wisdom supporting the *kavanah* of a trustee on the journey to mastery goes well beyond Jewish wisdom, religion, and spirituality. Another source is Spiral Dynamics. The trustee often best approaches his trust with an intention of "big mind." That is, a generous understanding and acceptance of the stage of the participants and the situation, as well as of the conflicts between the respective stages.

Like Maslow's hierarchy stretching from survival to self-actualization, which was one of its sources, Spiral Dynamics is a

chart of awareness and consciousness. Like personality profiles, Spiral Dynamics offers insights as to an individual's worldview and method of operation. Like grounded spirituality, Spiral Dynamics envisions a realm of consciousness that relates to a generative mindset: one that operates from understanding, unity, nonviolence, and open-mindedness.

Jay Hughes offers the best practice of thinking about one's trust client families every day with a Spiral Dynamics' big mind. One key perspective that distinguishes the big mind is acknowledging that the system is always bigger than we think it is. The cumulative impact can be one effective insight guided by compassion and not judgment.

The Pursuit of Happiness – and Emerging Science.

The *kavanah* of the master trustee is grounded in science. In fact, one of the thrilling thrusts of current science involves the study of accessing increased happiness. Consider the study by attorney Timothy O'Sullivan which concluded that, of all the factors and actors involved in the intergenerational transition, the one with a great, if not the greatest, impact on family happiness is the trustee.[13] Thus, the master trustee is mindful of his impact on the happiness of the family.

The depth of the action steps which naturally follow from this intention of creating happiness is revealed by another current scientific trend. These are the studies in neuroscience showing our ability to shape and even remake our physical as well as emotional

---

13 You can find more of Timothy O'Sullivan' thoughts in his 2007 article "Family Harmony: an all too frequent casualty of the estate planning process" in the Marquette Elder's Advisor.

selves. Among those in the forefront have included Dr. Davidson and his team at the University of Wisconsin – Madison, whose work included studying the Dali Lama's long-term meditation practice.

The master trustee employs practices that build from these findings. These practices inform the trustee's engagement, and can manifest in additional activities, especially those which tend to create culture, such as family ritual. This critical role of culture in dynamic tension with structure is explored later in the book.

Getting Under the Table with the Family.

I list here two other mastery practices which follow from *kavanah*. The first is well illustrated by a short story. The parents were exasperated with their young son who refused to come out from under the dining room table. The various experts they hired had no better luck enticing, ordering or otherwise influencing the child to leave his station under the table. Perhaps it was the master trustee, who when he was brought in, proceeded to get down on all fours and crawl under the dining room table with the boy. They spent a good amount of time talking to and sharing with each other, and both eventually came out from under the table. The point, of course, is that the trustee needs to get under the table with the stakeholders.

In other words, applying *kavanah* to the old adage to meet someone where they are.

Another best practice is for the master trustee to engage each beneficiary in setting the purpose of the trust for himself. Whether

or not the trust creator has set a purpose, the beneficiary is free to choose how he thinks of and experiences the trust. This can be an especially welcome practice, given that many beneficiaries underappreciate their power of contextualizing the trust. In fact, with the right *kavanah*, a master trustee can significantly enhance the beneficiary's power.

The application of *kavanah* informs the duty of loyalty and so deepens the six core practices as well as the twelve additional practices. Specifically, *kavanah* adds warmth and vision to these best practices, guiding their context and how they may be best considered and executed. This is especially true as to how a trustee may be advised to best practice loyalty.

I further suggest that the core practices of building trust as well as fostering growth are elements of *kavanah*. In other words, part of the *kavanah* of the master trustee is to build trust and foster growth.

Let's move forward informed by *kavanah*.

Chapter Ten
Polarity Thinking

A Case to Contemplate

Tom, the trustee, felt challenged in handling the distribution request from Betty, the beneficiary. While the trust allowed his discretion in supporting Betty's formal education, Betty's request was for funds so she could participate in classes as well as informal gatherings to develop her "heart-felt intuition."

Tom knew that Betty's father, Calvin, in creating this trust would have never allowed for her pursuit of a subject so far from the straight and narrow, so he felt the conflict between what Betty wanted to receive and what Calvin intended to give in the trust.

What should Tom do? What should he decide and how should he decide it?

This apparent conflict is the manifestation of an interdependent pair. For trustees, interdependent pairs have been observed as dualities. In fact, various authorities in the trustscape have long acknowledged the trustee's need to manage seemingly opposing forces. The apparent conflict between honoring the wishes of the trust creator on the one hand, and in empowering the beneficiary on the other, is but one example of many of such dualities for the trustee.

A trustee necessarily addresses the interdependent pair consisting of the trust creator's wishes on the one side and, on the other, the needs of the beneficiary. Each component of the pair is essential to successful trust administration, and neither is sufficient on its own. This is the definition of an interdependent pair.

It's no wonder that the trustee's job has been likened to the Roman god Janus – whose two faces could gaze on opposite perspectives simultaneously. How the better to consider simultaneously the grantor's vision from the past and the beneficiary's needs and wants for the future. As the Jewish theologian and philosopher Abraham Joshua Heschel once pointed out, this "polarity is an essential trait of all things. Tension, contrast, and contradiction characterize all of reality. … To ignore the paradox is to miss the truth."

And this truth leads us to the helpful methodology of *Polarity Thinking,* which offers a means to leverage the interdependencies inherent in the trustscape. This powerful methodology is a systematic approach for dealing with the duality inherent in the job of trust administration. The premise of Polarity Thinking applies to all aspects of reality. Our concern and focus are its application in the trustscape.

The term "interdependency" can relate to a pair or larger group. I'll use that term interchangeably with "polarity," "duality," and "dilemma." I'll avoid the use of the related term "opposite" for three reasons. First, because of its imprecision in describing both the absence or presence of one of the pairs in addition to referring

to the opposing natures of the pair. Second, it's rare that perfect opposites are present. Third, opposites are used in the Hegelian formula of the dialectic to lead to a single synthesis. The point of Polarity Thinking, in contrast, is to continue to utilize both poles. In other words, neither the Hegelian thesis nor antithesis disappear, but instead both remain in the Polarity Thinking model as essential ongoing components. I'll also avoid the use of the related term "paradox" because that relates to logical conundrums more than to interdependent pairs.

This chapter aims to introduce the reader to Polarity Thinking in the trustscape, including consideration of five core dualities of trusts.

- *Honoring the wishes of the trust creator while simultaneously empowering the beneficiary.*

- *Administering for the benefit of each individual beneficiary and all the beneficiaries as a group.*

- *Stewarding assets, particularly managing and taking care of both current as well as future distributions.*

- *Trustee communications which take into account the simultaneous needs for security and discretion as well as sharing and transparency.*

- *The trustee's loyalty to himself and his values AND[14] to the stakeholders of the trust.*

---

14 We'll use the fully capitalized word AND to highlight the special relationship and connection of interdependent pairs.

We'll first consider Polarity Thinking, and then address these five dualities. We'll then mention some additional dualities in the trustscape and add some observations. This is a deep dive, because the concept is new to most, and because the insights are large.

Polarity Thinking and its Application to the Trustscape.

Duality, the root of Polarity Thinking, can be found in ancient wisdom from various traditions. One conspicuous example comes from Taoism. The symbol of Yin and Yang is an instant and graphic portrayal of duality. Indeed, the essential of masculine and feminine energies can be an important element of all polarities, which is something we'll return to.

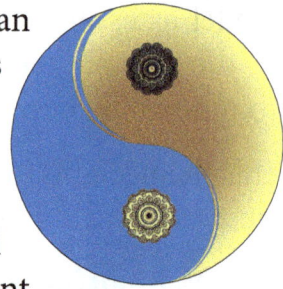

Another historic source of Polarity Thinking is the application of "on the other hand" thinking, which arises out of Jewish wisdom.

An instructive example of which appears in the Jewish Talmud in the discussion of when it is appropriate to pray. The discussion follows an oscillation of considerations, particularly between the alternative concepts that, on the one side, there are positives in praying regularly at set times and, on the other hand, praying during crisis or other specific need is also vitally important. This example is one of the central polarities according to Rabbi Abraham Joshua Heschel, in his book, Man's Quest for God.

Another example of a fundamental duality from Jewish wisdom: A person should carry a small stone in each pocket as reminders:

one, to remind you that the universe was created for you, the other to remind that in the scheme of things you have no significance. The art is, of course, when to reach for one reminder and when for the other.[15] Allowing for the engagement of kavanah, this is exactly the methodology that Polarity Thinking addresses.

The art, science, and practice of understanding and working with dualities, advanced significantly in 1975 with the publication of the book, *Polarity Management: Identifying and Managing Unsolvable Problems* by Barry Johnson, whose teaching and influence continues worldwide into the succeeding generation of advisors. Of additional interest here, Barry Johnson adopted the term polarity from the writings of Heschel.

The gist of Polarity Thinking is to manifest the best of interdependent pairs.[16] It entails both/and thinking, given that both the parts of the pairs (also known as "poles") are good and essential, and neither is sufficient on its own. In fact, it's the mistaken belief that one pole must be chosen over the other that often leads to the result which everyone wanted to avoid. So, in our example, if Tom simply decides that the trust language is the trust language, he's alienated Betty, the person who he's supposed

---

15 The root of this is in the two versions of creation. As described by Heschel, "There are two ways in which the Bible speaks of the creation of man. In the first chapter of the Book of Genesis, which is devoted to the creation of the physical universe, man is described as having been created in the image and likeness of God. In the second chapter, which tells us of the commandment not to eat of the fruit of the tree of knowledge, man is described as having been formed out of the dust of the earth. Together, image and dust express the interdependency of the nature of man. He is formed simultaneously of the most inferior stuff in the most superior image."

16 Of course, besides being found in certain pairs, interdependency is found in triads, quartets, and other combinations. Interdependent pairs form a core part of reality, encompassing masculine and feminine as well as yin and yang, to name just two foundational and omnipresent pairs. We will address other combinations particularly in the next chapter on the Five Energies.

to care for and protect. Worse, Betty may seek redress in court. On the other hand, if Tom simply throws up his hands and says, "whatever you want, Betty," he has violated the trust that Calvin put in him, and the law as well.

Choosing one or the other is called *either/or* thinking, which is also essential. There's no *both/and* thinking to apply to a question such as: "Who was the first president of the United States." Polarity Thinking is a supplement to *either/or* thinking, not a replacement for it.

Polarity Thinking helps in the choosing of which of the competing values should be followed in any particular moment, and so also supports the application of Practical Wisdom. More than the meaning of its descriptive words, the art of Practical Wisdom is the appreciation that all of us need to select from competing values in order to successfully navigate the complexity of the world around us. This helpful idea goes back to Aristotle and is the basis for the informative eponymous book by Barry Schwartz and Ken Sharpe.

Various experts have rightly suggested the application of Practical Wisdom to the trustscape. Consider one example of Practical Wisdom which resonates with trust administration: the scenario of a babysitter who references the parents' note clipped to the family refrigerator. That baby sitter is supposed to follow the parents' directions for the baby's schedule. And he is also expected to be mindful of the immediate needs of the baby.

So, consider one of the myriads of factual permutations: what if the baby is not yet interested in her 5 o'clock bottle as her designated

p.m. bedtime approaches? Should the sitter put the baby to bed at the directed time without the bottle, or should the bottle and bed be delayed until whenever the baby is ready? The babysitter has to apply Practical Wisdom to resolve the dilemma of which value – adherence to the appointed schedule or deference to the needs of the baby – he should follow.

A trustee, like the babysitter in the example, may be able to reach out to others for further guidance. Yet, for the trustee in pursuit of mastery, the key question is what methodology illuminates the selection of the value to be pursued. Practical Wisdom does not offer an express methodology to determine how to select between competing values. In fact, the implicit approach from the book is that only by engaging in a conscientious and aware practice over many years will the practitioner eventually develop proficiency at Practical Wisdom.

And perhaps by dint of experience, many trustees have developed successful approaches for dealing with the interdependent pairs inherent in trust administration. By definition, however, these approaches are idiosyncratic and based on a subjective and often unconscious competence.

While experience remains an important teacher, an express methodology can be an important tool and more efficient teacher. Polarity Thinking is one express methodology for balancing, if not positively leveraging interdependent pairs.

The methodology of Polarity Thinking employs a Polarity Map.®[17] The Polarity Map® holds various information around the upsides and feared downsides of each pole, as well as lists of action steps toward obtaining those upsides and warning signs of the down. Given its structure, the Map can help reveal aspects of the dilemma to the stakeholders involved and facilitates a shift in focus by revealing the energetic system involved. This energetic flow is simply and marvelously apparent as an infinity loop, a flow that oscillates from one pole to another.

Building on the work of Barry Johnson, Polarity Thinking moved closer to the trustscape with the publication of *Family Business as Paradox* by Amy Schuman and her colleagues John L. Ward and Stacy Stutz. This work identified several polarities which often appear in the trustscape as well as in the context of family businesses, including "family AND business" and "tradition AND change" and "harvest AND invest," as well as the tensions between the generations generally. We'll return to a few of these later.

Touching back briefly on what we've covered: Note that intention AND action constitute an interdependent pair themselves. And so, the *kavanah* in administering a particular trust is in oscillation with action.

Similarly, there are interdependent pairs enmeshed in the six core practices. Further, several of the 12 practices flowing from loyalty

---

17 Polarity Maps® are the excellent creation of Barry Johnson and his present organization, including his wisdom community. Polarity Map® is a registered trademark of Barry Johnson & Polarity Partnerships, LLC. Commercial use encouraged with permission®.

form interdependent pairs, namely: being meticulous AND considering the big picture, delivering results AND honoring process, and being honest and transparent AND exercising prudence and discretion. We'll return to these – and the last we'll look at in greater detail, given that communications rank high in importance in the trustscape.

A Deeper look at the Five Core Dualities in the Trustscape.

We'll now consider the five aforementioned key interdependent core duality pairs in the trustscape. These five are:

The trust creator's wishes AND the needs of the beneficiaries.

The fundamental polarity in the trustscape is the trust's need for honoring the wishes of the trust creator while simultaneously demanding empowerment of the beneficiary. The trust creator's wishes are expressed in the trust and sometimes in directives and other documents. The trustee manifests these wishes often when the trust creator is no longer available because of disability or death. In contrast, the needs of the beneficiaries are typically not recorded or given any systematic means of expression. To remedy this silent voice is yet another reason for creating mission statements, goals, and distribution policies with beneficiaries.

Trust administration that addresses only the needs of the beneficiaries may well dishonor or even violate the wishes of the trust creator set out in the trust documents. On the other hand, ignoring the impact of the trust on the beneficiaries is a key source of friction and litigation – and why some 80% of trust beneficiaries

consider their trusts to be a burden, according to Jay Hughes. In fact, the blind application of the trust creator's document to the destruction of the beneficiaries exalts form over substance and in so doing, dishonors the trust creator's typical (if too often merely implicit) intention to bless the beneficiaries. Trust expert Hartley Goldstone has well identified this known negative problem as "The Trustee who Mistook his Checklist for Wisdom."

Of course, every trust creator may not always intend to bless the beneficiary. A trust creator may intend to punish the beneficiary in some way. The trustee then has the decision as to whether to participate in that punishment, including, but perhaps not limited to, whether to serve as trustee.

Even without the lens of Polarity Thinking, good trust administration remains at least mindful of the impact on the beneficiaries. Think of the trustee as the captain of a ship with the trust document as his directions. In the act of navigating, the captain must necessarily also consider the impact of the ship's wake as well as the health and safety of his crew. We would not have much respect for a captain who capsized other ships or abused his crew, even if he's successful in bringing the ship to the appointed harbor.

Polarity Thinking can help a *good* trustee who is merely mindful to walk on the road to *mastery* by administering the trust to improve the lives of the beneficiaries. As we discussed in our section on *kavanah*, the master trustee works to empower the beneficiaries in as many ways as possible. More precisely, Polarity

Thinking helps make possible the professional dynamic balancing of this duality of honoring the wishes of the trust creator while empowering the beneficiaries.

Consider the Polarity Map® presented in Image A detailing one expression of the core trust polarity: the wishes or gifts of the trust creator AND their receipt by the beneficiary.

Trust Gift AND Receipt Polarity Map®

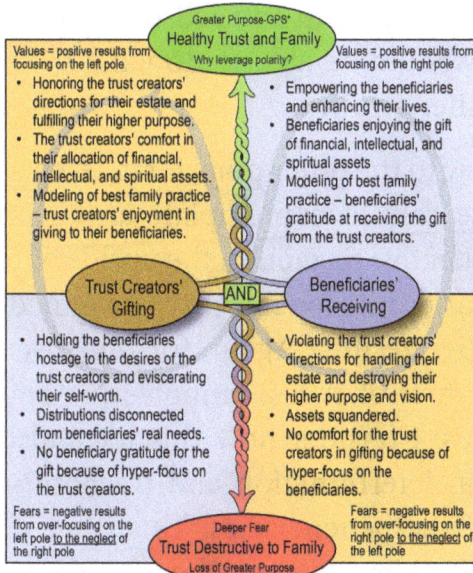

Action Steps

How will we gain or maintain the positive results from focusing on this left pole? What? Who? By When? Measures?

1. Trust Creator/Trustee:
   A. Articulate trust purpose/ mission/vision.
   B. Anticipate and plan and field test trust impact.
   C. Create stewardship policy, procedures, and budgets.
2. Trustee/Trust Creator/ Beneficiaries adopt communication system.

Early Warnings***

Measurable indicators (things you can count) that will let you know that you are getting into the downside of this left pole.

A. Trust creators ignore the impact of the gift.
B. Trust creators ignore the beneficiaries' freedom and independent vision.
C. Beneficiaries' complaints.
D. No express beneficiary vision or "buy-in."

Greater Purpose-GPS*
Healthy Trust and Family
Why leverage polarity?

Values = positive results from focusing on the left pole
Values = positive results from focusing on the right pole

- Honoring the trust creators' directions for their estate and fulfilling their higher purpose.
- The trust creators' comfort in their allocation of financial, intellectual, and spiritual assets.
- Modeling of best family practice – trust creators' enjoyment in giving to their beneficiaries.

- Empowering the beneficiaries and enhancing their lives.
- Beneficiaries enjoying the gift of financial, intellectual, and spiritual assets
- Modeling of best family practice – beneficiaries' gratitude at receiving the gift from the trust creators.

Trust Creators' Gifting   AND   **Beneficiaries' Receiving**

- Holding the beneficiaries hostage to the desires of the trust creators and eviscerating their self-worth.
- Distributions disconnected from beneficiaries' real needs.
- No beneficiary gratitude for the gift because of hyper-focus on the trust creators.

- Violating the trust creators' directions for handling their estate and destroying their higher purpose and vision.
- Assets squandered.
- No comfort for the trust creators in gifting because of hyper-focus on the beneficiaries.

Fears = negative results from over-focusing on the left pole to the neglect of the right pole

Fears = negative results from over-focusing on the right pole to the neglect of the left pole

Deeper Fear
Trust Destructive to Family
Loss of Greater Purpose

Action Steps

How will we gain or maintain the positive results from focusing on this right pole? What? Who? By When? Measures?

Trustee/Beneficiaries:

A. Create trust mission/vision.
B. Revisit impact of trust and administration regularly.
C. Monitor and discuss asset stewardship policy, procedures, and budgets.
D. Adopt communication system.

Early Warnings

Measurable indicators (things you can count) that will let you know that you are getting into the downside of this right pole.

A. Beneficiaries do not consider the opportunity of the gift.
B. Beneficiaries do not understand or "buy-in" to the trust creator's vision.
C. Addiction and other dysfunction.
D. Disregard of the provisions of the trust document.

Polarity Map © 1992, 2008 Polarity Partnerships, LLC
Map Content © 2015, 2024 Felix Group, P.C.

Image A: This Polarity Map® identifies the two poles in the ovals as the polarity of Gifting and Receiving to achieve the Greater Purpose of achieving both a healthy trust and family.

See immediately the contrasting nature of these two. As illustrated in our opening story of Tom Trustee and Betty Beneficiary, focus

on the wishes of Calvin the Trust Creator forms a polarity with the impact of those wishes on Betty the Beneficiary.

The Polarity Map® details the values in the two positive upper quadrants for each pole. Specifically, for our purposes, I've posited three separate positive values that flow from focusing on the Trust Creator's Gifting. For our purposes, let's just look at the first one, namely: Honoring the trust creator's directions for handling his affairs and estate. This value reflects our culture's high esteem for the principles of freedom and self-determination, specifically, that individuals should be able to do what they want with their assets and their life.

Change focus now to the other pole. First, let's acknowledge again the polarity: one cannot contemplate an effective gift without considering an effective receipt. In the upside of the consideration of the Beneficiaries' Receiving I've imagined three possible values and positive results. Again, for our discussion here, let's look only at the first of those: empowering and enhancing the beneficiaries' lives. Consider how this ideal also resonates with the values of self-determination and freedom – although from the viewpoint of the beneficiaries. This is an illustration of the power of a Polarity Map® to force the consideration of the values and results flowing from recognition of interdependent pairing. The counter-intuitive result: achieving the upside of one pole is dependent on going to the upside of the other. *In other words, the only way to achieve the trust creator's vision is to also consider how the trust will improve the lives of the beneficiaries.*

To the extent the reader understands and accepts the science around interdependent pairs assembled in Polarity Thinking as immutable, the reader will accept the conclusion that this science *requires* a trustee to engage in blessing the beneficiaries and *forbids* him to blindly apply the words of the trust against the beneficiary. This premise imposes on the trustee an obligation above the legal minimum requirements to serve the beneficiary and may lead him to take steps to soften the application of the trust's language to the extent permissible under the law and reasonable under the circumstances.

In addition to detailing the positive values of the poles, the expression of the downsides of these values is equally as important. This Polarity Map® displays the fears and negative results in the two lower quadrants – at the bottom, the deeper fear: a dysfunctional, destructive trust. Over-focus on the gift of the trust creator to the neglect of how the beneficiaries may receive it may result in any of the three distinct fears listed. Let's just discuss the first one: Holding the beneficiaries hostage to the past and eviscerating their self-worth. This fear is likely common, given the stereotypical pull of the trust creator as the gravitational force of the family system. As articulated by the authors of *The Voice of the Rising Generation*, the strong force of the trust creator, even after his physical removal from the system, often limits the beneficiaries to the pull of the trust creator's past brilliance.

On the other pole, namely, the overfocus on the receiving by the beneficiaries to the exclusion of the wishes of the trust creator, I've posited three other fears and negative results that the trust creator likely may hold. Again, we'll discuss here only the first of those three: Violating the trust creator's directions for handling his affairs and estate and destroying his higher purpose. That is to say that a trust creator may reasonably fear that an overfocus on his beneficiaries may lead to a disregard of his directions and vision.

Another practical insight from the application of Polarity Thinking: the stronger one values one side, the greater the fear in being caught in the downside of the other pole. Recognition of those fears and possible downsides is essential for successfully leveraging polarities. It is simply insufficient to focus only on the benefits of the respective values; we need to acknowledge the negatives as well.

Moving to the outer margins of this Polarity Map®, note at the top of the left and right side a list of Action Steps that are reasonably calculated to accomplish what's detailed in the adjacent upper positive quadrants. So, consider the first of the Action Steps imagined in this example for the trustee to accomplish the gift of the trust creator, specifically: "The Trust Creator articulating (and the Trustee manifesting) his trust purpose/mission/vision." As it happily happens, the trust creator's act of expressing his purpose, mission, and vision for his trust is a logical, practical step to accomplish not just the first, but all three of the positive results contemplated in the pole of the Trust Creator's Gifting. To

the extent that the trust creator has not articulated his purpose, mission, and goals, it becomes the opportunity for the trustee to articulate them as appropriate.

In addition, this Action Step of expressing the trust creator's purpose is logically a step to *avoid* the *fear* of the trust creator of overfocus on the beneficiaries. Recall this fear is expressed in the downside of Beneficiaries Receiving pole.

On that Beneficiaries Receiving pole, I've listed four Action Steps, which might reasonably help the trustee to accomplish the values and positive results of Receiving by the Beneficiaries. For our discussion, let's look for a moment just at the first Action Step on this side of the Polarity Map®: The Trustee and Beneficiaries co-creating and implementing or adopting the trust's mission/vision *for them.*

Consider how the action of the beneficiaries adopting their own purpose, mission or vision for the trust is reasonably calculated to achieve the positive result of having the trust improve their lives. Consider how this action step is also reasonably calculated to address the first listed *fear* of the beneficiaries: being held hostage to the past.

The beneficiaries' articulating their purpose for the trust is not often considered in the practice of trust administration. Revealing previously unknown solutions such as this again illustrates the power of a Polarity Map.®

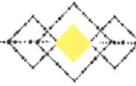

Further, as may be fitting to the situation, the trust creator can engage the beneficiaries on both the purpose, mission, and vision of the trust for him and for them. In this way, the family may gain additional traction because the family may more consciously and more collaboratively create on behalf of the entire family. This is family work that can be done even before the Trustee is hired. And, of course, easier said than done.

Moving to the last of the elements of this Polarity Map,® I've detailed four possible Early Warnings for both sets of the feared results. Starting on the left side of the Polarity Map,® the four Early Warnings express possible manifestations of the beneficiaries' fears of an overfocus on the trust creator to their exclusion. Let's again consider the first one in this list: the trust creator ignoring the impact of the gift. In other words, the trust creator's lack of willingness to simply consider the impact of his gift on the beneficiaries may logically be a red flag that the trust will end up holding the beneficiaries hostage to the past, and not help improve their lives. Where a trust creator has considered the impact, this particular Early Warning might be expressed as failure to *fully* consider the impact of his gift. What may constitute "full consideration" will vary from family to family.

This failure is a key current flaw in the creation of trusts. The result of this flaw is often painful and sometimes fatal, given how it is naturally magnified in administration. Worse, the trust creator's consideration is typically one-sided: he limits his assessment of

the impact to his own thinking, rarely soliciting input from the beneficiaries or even from an expert trustee.

In my practice, I've been asked to assist with numerous trusts which have each failed mightily in their respective way to consider the impact of the trust creator's vision on the administration on behalf of the beneficiaries. Some of these trusts are so flawed that the first order of business on the death of the trust creator is to reform the trust to make it workable.[18]

Polarity Thinking helps expose this flaw. The current cultural experience is that the trust creation process is one exclusively focused on the trust creator. The trust creator hires the trust and estate attorney, who by force of law is bound to manifest the vision of the trust creator, and likely cannot place the needs of the beneficiaries above those of his client. Some more enlightened trust-drafting attorneys will help their client consider the impact, and even help make the trust more purposeful. Even these approaches do not fully address the need. I've experienced far too few attorneys who are open to at least a once over of the trust by the trustee. In the design of an airplane, it is hard to imagine the engineers would not consider the input from the pilot's point of

---

18 For those concerned with the technicalities: such reformations can be accomplished in a number of ways, perhaps easiest when the trustee, trust protector, or other trust fiduciary are extended the power in the trust document to accomplish the needed change. In Illinois, this process generally involves a Nonjudicial Settlement Agreement (which is simply an agreement of all the pertinent trust stakeholders). In certain situations, such reformation may need to be accomplished through a formal *decanting* or rewriting of the trust or via court order. The time and expense of any of these varies greatly by situation.

view. In the trustscape, it is the inadequate norm for the trustee to take his first test drive during the maiden voyage, that is, after the death of the trust creator.

I know of fewer attorneys who encourage the potential beneficiaries to test drive the trust that is being designed for them. There is some hope. Having experienced the breakdown for the prior generation or witnessed their neighbors trust traumas, more families are open to this service. But if my practice is representative, the number of families taking this ounce of prevention is a tiny minority.

Given the premise that trust creators generally desire to bless their beneficiaries, enlightened trustees and advisors may be able to educate others, and thus positively leverage to avoid this realistic fear.

We move to the right side of the Polarity Map® to sample an Early Warning of the appearance of any of the four possible fears of the trust creator, which I've posited in the event of over focusing on the beneficiaries to his exclusion. The first possible Warning is "the beneficiaries do not consider the opportunity of the gift." In other words, the failure of the beneficiaries to consider how the trust might benefit them may reasonably indicate the trust creator's fears may come to pass. For example, beneficiaries who see no gift may be more prone to violate the trust creator's vision, because they simply don't recognize a value in honoring that vision. Of course, given that the creation of the trust starts with

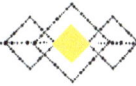

the trust creator, leveraging his real and understandable fears may be the more efficient door to create a more successful trust.

During active trust administration, the appearance of one or more of the Warnings may be an indication of a hyper focus on one of the poles to the exclusion of the other. The trustee should consider investigating further to see where the breakdown may be. That investigation could be an investigation of the quality of the execution of the Actions Steps for the other pole. If those Action Steps are being performed, the trustee may look to other solutions, such as adopting other Action Steps, which may more reasonably accomplish the upside of that pole.

Finally, the infinity loop reflects the proven wisdom of Polarity Thinking that ongoing acts of respecting the poles will appear at least energetically as an oscillation between the upsides of both the poles, incorporating the best of both, and minimizing the encounters with the negative.

Of course, all the content inside the Polarity Map® – the intentions, the values, the fears, the results, the action steps, and the early warnings – may be expressed differently depending on the trustee and the stakeholders involved. That includes the expression of the polarity itself. However, a Polarity Map® dealing with this particular duality will likely have some resemblance to this sample.

The above Polarity Map® (Image A) and example assumed that the trustee and the beneficiary were different individuals, such as parent and child. As an alternative example, consider the situation

where the trustee and the beneficiary are the same person, such as an individual preparing for impending disability. The expression of this Polarity Map® would highlight more the dilemma of the wisdom of the trustee's judgment AND the expression of the wishes of the trust creator/beneficiary. One manifestation of that would be dealing with the latter's desires to be maintained at his home while the trustee perceives impracticality in providing home care.

Again, the content of any Polarity Map® will vary depending on the situation and the people involved. In fact, ALL of the language appearing on the Polarity Map® may be best written by the trustee and applicable stakeholders in the moment. That's because the Polarity Map® is a dynamic reflection of reality and not an academic exercise.

Despite the detail in this Polarity Map,® it also shortcuts the reality around multiple beneficiaries, simply because every human beneficiary is an individual with different personalities, needs, goals, and situations. Thus, in addition to an overall Polarity Map® which follows the outline of this one, the master trustee should also create individual Polarity Maps® of this trustee AND beneficiary polarity for each beneficiary.

The Trustscape Interdependency of Individual AND Multiple Beneficiaries.

In addition to the interdependency of the "trust creator AND beneficiary," there exists the interdependency of "particular beneficiary AND all beneficiaries." This polarity is especially common in the administration of so-called pot trusts, where

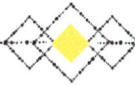

distributions to multiple beneficiaries are to be made from a common fund. In these pot-trust situations, the trustee must consider both the needs of the beneficiaries as a whole group as well as the needs of each individual beneficiary. Of course, as always, the trustee's consideration is shaped by the language and terms of the trust document AND the dynamics of each individual trustscape in the context of this inherent interdependency.

A specific distribution request of a particular beneficiary must be considered in respect to the needs of the others as well as to the group as a whole. In addition to taking these into consideration, the trustee may have duties to communicate accordingly. So, for example, the trustee may have the legal if not moral duty to advise the other beneficiaries of any distribution to one beneficiary. It could also be helpful for the trustee to be able to reference the policy for the whole, which he has applied to the one beneficiary – and then, would presumably also apply to the benefit of the others in their turn.

Thus, the interdependency of "beneficiary AND all the beneficiaries" relates to the interdependency of "individual AND family." A trustee may be called upon to think about the overall direction and benefit of the family at large. At the same time, supporting the family is recognized as serving the individual needs of each family member.

These polarities dealing with a subgroup and the entire group resonate with the universal interdependency of "part AND whole." *A known feature of this interdependency is that deeply*

and positively being in the particular part can enable the whole to be more powerful – and vice-versa. Appropriate care of the individual beneficiary enhances the care of the beneficiaries as a whole, especially while also administrating to take care of the beneficiaries as a group, as denoted in Image B. Peter White offers a fine spiritual expression of this counter-intuitive wisdom: "Miraculously, the greater the soul's experience of unity, the greater the soul's experience of individuality…. We are the lake and the unique within it."

Beneficiary AND Beneficiaries Polarity Map®

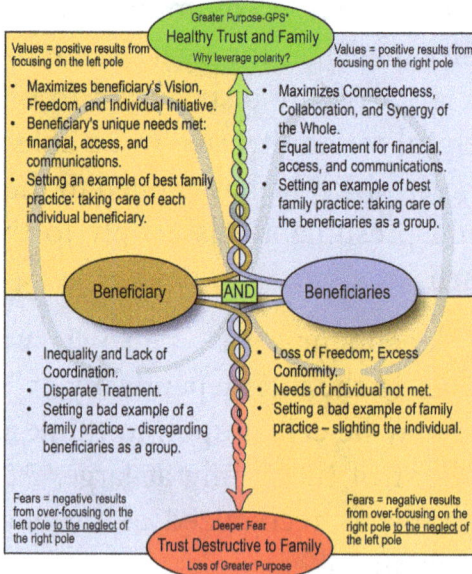

Action Steps
How will we gain or maintain the positive results from focusing on this left pole? What? Who? By When? Measures?

Trustee/Beneficiary create for each individual beneficiary:

1. Trust purpose/mission/vision statement.
2. Trust stewardship policy, procedures, and budgets.
3. Communication system for each beneficiary.
4. Legacy plan.

Greater Purpose-GPS* — Healthy Trust and Family
Why leverage polarity?

Values = positive results from focusing on the left pole

- Maximizes beneficiary's Vision, Freedom, and Individual Initiative.
- Beneficiary's unique needs met: financial, access, and communications.
- Setting an example of best family practice: taking care of each individual beneficiary.

Values = positive results from focusing on the right pole

- Maximizes Connectedness, Collaboration, and Synergy of the Whole.
- Equal treatment for financial, access, and communications.
- Setting an example of best family practice: taking care of the beneficiaries as a group.

Action Steps
How will we gain or maintain the positive results from focusing on this right pole? What? Who? By When? Measures?

Trustee/Beneficiaries create for all beneficiaries as a group:

1. Trust purpose/mission/vision statement.
2. Trust stewardship policy, procedures, and budgets.
3. Communication system.
4. Legacy plan.

Beneficiary AND **Beneficiaries**

Early Warnings*
Measurable indicators (things you can count) that will let you know that you are getting into the downside of this left pole.

A. Complaints about how the group of beneficiaries are being treated.
B. Disregarding the trust creator's memory and vision about the beneficiaries as a whole.
C. No beneficiary group vision.
D. No group beneficiary "buy-in."
E. Poor trustee/beneficiaries communications.

- Inequality and Lack of Coordination.
- Disparate Treatment.
- Setting a bad example of a family practice – disregarding beneficiaries as a group.

- Loss of Freedom; Excess Conformity.
- Needs of individual not met.
- Setting a bad example of family practice – slighting the individual.

Early Warnings
Measurable indicators (things you can count) that will let you know that you are getting into the downside of this right pole.

A. Complaints about how individual beneficiaries are being treated.
B. Lack of power or purpose of individual beneficiaries.
C. Addiction and other dysfunction.
D. Lack of "buy-in" by individual beneficiary.
E. Poor trustee/beneficiary communications

Fears = negative results from over-focusing on the left pole to the neglect of the right pole

Fears = negative results from over-focusing on the right pole to the neglect of the left pole

Deeper Fear — Trust Destructive to Family
Loss of Greater Purpose

Polarity Map © 1992, 2008 Polarity Partnerships, LLC
Map Content © 2015, 2024 Felix Group, P.C.

Image B: *This Polarity Map® identifies the two poles in the ovals as the polarity of Beneficiary AND Beneficiaries to achieve the Greater Purpose of achieving both a healthy trust and family.*

The Action Steps and Early Warnings for this Polarity Map® remain similar, relying on a robust and accepted stewardship policy as well as trust-building communications for success. The difference is that the trustee has addressed the policy and communications for BOTH the individual beneficiary as well as to the group of beneficiaries as a whole. Again, applying the counter-intuitive positive result of Polarity Thinking: only in managing both the individual and the group can the trustee set the trust up for the highest success with either.

As it happens, both the Action Steps of the trustee's communications and the trust's stewardship policies necessarily invoke interdependent pairs of their own. This is a prime example of a nested pair, the known phenomenon of an interdependent pair residing in another interdependent pair.

Need/Achievement AND Blood/Equality. An important interdependent pair which often appears along with multiple beneficiaries concerns what the beneficiaries may enjoy on account of their need or merit AND that which flows to them simply from being a member of the family, for example, in treating all equally. This interdependency presents in many places in the trustscape. One of its first appearances is in the trust creator's initial determination during the drafting of the trust document of who gets what. In that situation, there's one pole calling for division of the trust's assets to be split into equal shares, representing the equal claims of the family beneficiaries.

So, for example, if there are three surviving children of the trust creator, each should receive one-third of the trust.

On the other side of equal treatment is the consideration of need. So where two of those three beneficiaries are well off financially, the trust creator may be called to gift more to the less well-off third child. And there's the even more compelling variant where that third beneficiary is "special needs." Hence the idea reflected in the familiar phrase "fair is not necessarily equal."

Our current culture generally prioritizes equal treatment, except in the event of disability. Further, consideration of disability extends beyond legal incapacity to include the so-called ne'er-do-well offspring, who for whatever reason are not as facile with money as their siblings and particularly as their parent.

One reason identified for *not* having the capacity to accomplish wealth production is connected with intergenerational oscillation. This shift in generational talents is nicely featured by the story of John Rockefeller's Senior and Junior. The former was remarkable for accumulating riches and the latter spending through philanthropy. We discuss intergenerational oscillation further in a later chapter.

This disparity in beneficiary need calls for the trustee to address this as part of the discussions with the group of beneficiaries. The family will more successfully navigate this dilemma to the extent they can agree to give special attention to the beneficiary in greater need.

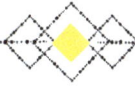

The flip side of need is achievement. Trusts are sometimes structured to reward certain achievements of the beneficiary. Sometimes this reward may be the only distribution available to the beneficiary. Sometimes it is structured as an extra incentive, among other scenarios. Where such trusts include multiple beneficiaries, the trustee may be well advised to address the incentives with both the individual beneficiaries as well as the beneficiaries as a group.

Finally, this Need/Achievement AND Blood/Equality often appears in the context of family businesses. The tension is over which family members may participate in the management or operations of the business as well as who may receive benefits and how much. No small issues. And the subject of an entire chapter in Schuman's book.

Because the trustee's stewardship policies are present in many if not most all trusts, we'll next consider them.

Interdependent Pairs Around Trust Asset Stewardship

There are a number of related polarities connecting to both the investment and the distribution of assets. These include variants on giving AND receiving, such as sowing AND reaping, as well as the paired considerations of current AND future needs. Another interdependent pair in this category is identified by Schuman as "harvest AND invest." However named, at its heart

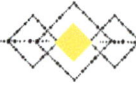

this interdependency is connected to the trustee's fundamental role of protector. The protection is often characterized as being active and dynamic, both in the present and over time. I'll refer to this category of polarities as asset stewardship, and we'll focus in on the current AND future needs interdependency specifically.

As a part of navigating these stewardship polarities, the master trustee should adopt a stewardship policy for both the investment and for the distribution of assets. This is true especially where the trustee has discretion over some or all of the investment and distribution decisions. Such policies serve as organizing structures around the intentions and actions of the trust as well as appropriately managing the expectations of the beneficiaries.

Current best practices invite a trustee to generate an Investment Policy Statement (IPS). An IPS is one part of the policy. Often there's a benefit in articulating the policies for distributions as well. In fact, where the trustee might be exercising his discretion in *denying* distribution requests of a beneficiary, it might be salutary to have the beneficiary invested in a coherent statement of what requests will be honored. The case of *Spencer v. DiCola*, for example, is instructive in that the trustee refused certain requests for distribution for beneficiary education on the grounds of wanting to save funds for later distribution, while apparently failing to offer a vision – let alone a compelling vision – of the later distributions and their benefits. The preparation of a Distribution Policy Statement is a best practice addressing the management of the finite amount of assets held by virtually all trusts.

A key challenge, of course, is that typically the needs and demands of the present are seen and felt more sharply and urgently by the beneficiaries than those of the future. Those needs, after all, are present now. Often the more distant that future – for example, a young adult contemplating his old age – the less compelling the urgency to address them. In fact, it may be difficult for a beneficiary to attach much importance to them whatsoever. The Polarity Map® is another tool for the trustee to help reveal the importance of future needs to the beneficiary. The creation of this Polarity Map® with beneficiaries can also help obtain their buy-in to an acceptable stewardship policy.

Repeating our finding that the trust documents are not the last words to the trustee, cocreation of the stewardship policy picks up where the trust documents leave off. Unless otherwise instructed by the documents, the trustee may have to consider both the current needs and wants of the beneficiary with reasonably projected later needs. Typically, the trust document does not dictate a stewardship policy, and so the master trustee assumes the responsibility and the opportunity to cocreate one.

As an example, a trust creator may direct through his document that the trust assets are to be used primarily to get a minor beneficiary through university. Without such directing language – typically trusts simply cloak the trustee with discretion – the trustee may have to actively manage this interdependency, which could lead to that same goal of getting the minor beneficiary a

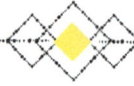

college degree. The significant difference: in the latter case, the beneficiary expressly adopts this goal.

The importance of cocreation of a stewardship policy cannot be overemphasized. Such a policy may reduce risk because of the documentation of the decision and perhaps also from the deeper acceptance by beneficiaries of policies which they cocreated. A Polarity Map® executed with the involvement of the beneficiary may be an essential tool to aid frank and difficult discussions of stewardship policies and decisions.

Current AND Future Needs Polarity Map®

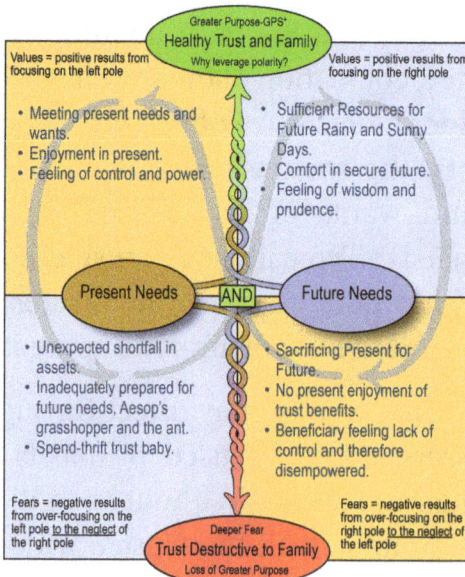

Action Steps

How will we gain or maintain the positive results from focusing on this left pole? What? Who? By When? Measures?

Trustee/Beneficiary engage current needs in creating:

1. Trust purpose/mission/vision statement.
2. Stewardship policy and procedures.
3. An annual budget.
4. Present scenario exercises.
5. Gratitude exercises.

Early Warnings*

Measurable indicators (things you can count) that will let you know that you are getting into the downside of this left pole.

A. No talk of lifetime budget outside of budget workshop.
B. No talk of future scenarios or delayed gratification outside of exercises.
C. Focus solely on spontaneous needs.
D. No demonstration of delayed gratification.

Greater Purpose-GPS*
Healthy Trust and Family
Why leverage polarity?

Values = positive results from focusing on the left pole

Values = positive results from focusing on the right pole

- Meeting present needs and wants.
- Enjoyment in present.
- Feeling of control and power.

- Sufficient Resources for Future Rainy and Sunny Days.
- Comfort in secure future.
- Feeling of wisdom and prudence.

Present Needs [AND] **Future Needs**

- Unexpected shortfall in assets.
- Inadequately prepared for future needs, Aesop's grasshopper and the ant.
- Spend-thrift trust baby.

- Sacrificing Present for Future.
- No present enjoyment of trust benefits.
- Beneficiary feeling lack of control and therefore disempowered.

Fears = negative results from over-focusing on the left pole to the neglect of the right pole

Fears = negative results from over-focusing on the right pole to the neglect of the left pole

Deeper Fear
Trust Destructive to Family
Loss of Greater Purpose

Action Steps

How will we gain or maintain the positive results from focusing on the right pole? What? Who? By When? Measures?

Trustee/Beneficiary engage future needs in creating:

1. Trust purpose/mission/vision statement.
2. Stewardship policy and procedures.
3. A lifetime budget.
4. Future scenario exercises.
5. Delayed gratification exercises.

Early Warnings

Measurable indicators (things you can count) that will let you know that you are getting into the downside of this right pole.

A. Absence of activity for the benefit in the present, e.g., too many NOs from the trustee.
B. Austerity without promise of future benefit, e.g., austerity for its own sake.

Polarity Map © 1992, 2008 Polarity Partnerships, LLC
Map Content © 2015, 2024 Felix Group, P.C.

Image C: *offers one expression of the Polarity Map® of current and future needs, using language and ideas which come from a mixture of my experience and study.*

Noteworthy on this Polarity Map® are the powerful actions available to a trustee to leverage this situation. Too often failures in the balancing of current and future needs are blamed on the beneficiary. In those situations, the beneficiary is shamed for his failure to have developed the unpopular and rare skill of delayed gratification and efficient budgeting.

In the nightmare scenario, the trustee's knee-jerk response is to insist all the more on the beneficiary's focus on a future-orientation, which typically causes the beneficiary to feel less in control, and less able or willing to be compliant. The end result of this vicious spiral downward is further dysfunction and destruction. While it's true that the beneficiary's engaged participation is essential to the success of any trust, it's also true that the trustee, as the professional in the room, should take the lead in activity reasonably calculated to produce a successful trust.

Legally, the trustee is held to the same fiduciary standards, despite his experience level and without consideration of whether the trustee is in the business of trust administration. Morally, trustees should be held to the same high standard, given the critical difference a trustee makes to the success of a trust. I do NOT think that Polarity Thinking is a minimum requirement of a trustee, but rather is a tool for a trustee who aspires to give his families far in excess of the minimum.

One key message from this Polarity Map®: only by engaging in the meaningful satisfaction of the present needs of the beneficiary may the trustee succeed in having the beneficiary address her future needs.

Let's change our attention to the different subject of the methods of trustee administration, specifically, the key interdependency around how the trustee communicates with the beneficiary around the values of Transparency AND Discretion.

The Trustscape Polarities Around Trustee and Beneficiary Communications.

The trustee's communications may embody the competing interests of Transparency AND Discretion. Naked transparency, that is, sharing which is not balanced by the trustee's protection of confidential and sensitive information, can be naïve and destructive. On the other hand, secrecy can foster distrust and hobble efficiency when not balanced by the natural need for stakeholders to know what is going on and so, can also be destructive. It is only in the dynamic leveraging of these two poles that the better course can be defined.

Thus, it may be seen that two of the dozen additional best practices we've previously discussed exist in this particular polar relationship. Specifically, the best practice of being "honest and transparent" is necessarily in dynamic balance with the best

practice of the trustee "exercising prudence and discretion." Ultimately, by the law of Polarity Thinking to accomplish either one of those, the trustee must necessarily engage the other.

Responsible Information Management Polarity Map®

Action Steps

How will we gain or maintain the positive results from focusing on this left pole? What? Who? By When? Measures?

1. Adopt communications policy and practice, including make-good for any deviation from policy.
2. Respond to queries and engage in periodic feedback loop.
3. Consider receiver's ability to hear, preferences, and expectations.
4. Consider communication's confidentiality, sensitivity, likely impact, desired result, timing, context, and cadence.

Early Warnings****

Measurable indicators (things you can count) that will let you know that you are getting into the downside of this left pole.

A. Non-disclosure of external operational info.
B. Questions indicating lack of information or lack of understanding of larger, foundations.
C. Use of outside professionals to request information.
D. Demonstration of fear from lack of knowledge.

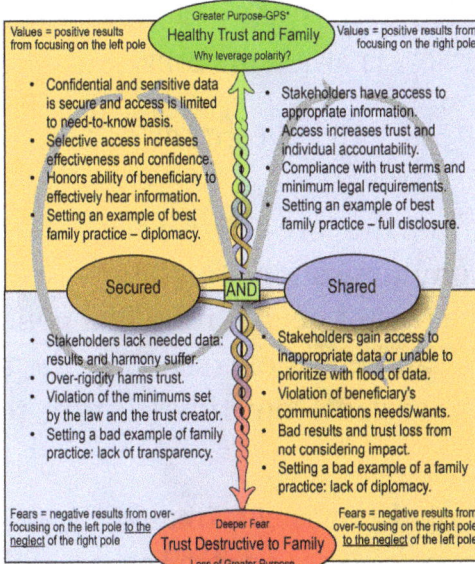

Greater Purpose-GPS*
Healthy Trust and Family
Why leverage polarity?

Values = positive results from focusing on the left pole

- Confidential and sensitive data is secure and access is limited to need-to-know basis.
- Selective access increases effectiveness and confidence.
- Honors ability of beneficiary to effectively hear information.
- Setting an example of best family practice – diplomacy.

Secured [AND] **Shared**

- Stakeholders lack needed data: results and harmony suffer.
- Over-rigidity harms trust.
- Violation of the minimums set by the law and the trust creator.
- Setting a bad example of family practice: lack of transparency.

Fears = negative results from over-focusing on the left pole to the neglect of the right pole

Deeper Fear
Trust Destructive to Family
Loss of Greater Purpose

Values = positive results from focusing on the right pole

- Stakeholders have access to appropriate information.
- Access increases trust and individual accountability.
- Compliance with trust terms and minimum legal requirements.
- Setting an example of best family practice – full disclosure.

- Stakeholders gain access to inappropriate data or unable to prioritize with flood of data.
- Violation of beneficiary's communications needs/wants.
- Bad results and trust loss from not considering impact.
- Setting a bad example of a family practice: lack of diplomacy.

Fears = negative results from over-focusing on the right pole to the neglect of the left pole

Action Steps

How will we gain or maintain the positive results from focusing on this right pole? What? Who? By When? Measures?

1. Adopt communications policy and practice, including make-good for any deviation from policy.
2. Respond to queries and engage in periodic feedback loop.
3. Communicate promptly and authentically.

Early Warnings

Measurable indicators (things you can count) that will let you know that you are getting into the downside of this right pole.

A. Demonstrations of hostility, being triggered and other highly emotional responses.
B. No strategy as to means manner of communication.
C. Unresponsive behavior due to failure to use appropriate communications.
D. Manipulative behavior due to failure to be prudent.

Polarity Map © 1992, 2008 Polarity Partnerships, LLC
Map Content © 2015, 2024 Felix Group, P.C.

Image D: *This Polarity Map® identifies the two poles in the ovals as the polarity of responsible information management to achieve the Greater Purpose of achieving both a healthy trust and family.*

Note the first two Action Steps on both poles are identical. Under Polarity Thinking, these actions deserve deep consideration because of their efficiency: they may be able to help accomplish

both sets of the desired results and avoid both sets of feared negative results.

These Steps are to…

- create and articulate a communication policy, including a "make good" program for any deviation from the communications policy, and

- engage in periodic feedback.

These steps flow from the core practice of the trustee to build trust and the use of communications to build trust and demonstrate loyalty. Should the trustee deviate from that policy, no matter the reason, the result can be loss of trust. How the trustee remedies any deviation is important, sometimes critical, to the restoration of trust.

The importance of the trustee's "making good" applies to his violation of any policy. This is a critical aspect of the trustee on the journey of mastery. A violation – however inadvertent – reflects on a trustee's loyalty, including his demonstrating each of the core practices. And so, the means and manner of addressing or curing that defect also invoke loyalty and the core practices. A simple acknowledgement of the deviation may be merely a first step. The best practice is to leverage the deviation into an opportunity for fostering growth – particularly for the trustee and, depending on

the situation, possibly for the beneficiary and other stakeholders as well.

Note a new feature in the last two of the Action Steps for gaining/ maintaining Secured Information: a list of factors to be addressed. These flow from the related interdependency of Intention AND Impact. The classic line shouted by Jack Nickolson's character in the 1992 movie, *a Few Good Men*, "You can't handle the truth," highlights the trustee's consideration of the component part of the Impact of a Particular Communication. In addition to the consideration of how the beneficiary will subjectively receive the information, impact also might include the legal significance of the communication, including how it looks as part of the trust's permanent record.

The other factors listed are not part of interdependent pairs themselves but are instead either/or choices. Let's consider a few of them.

Ability of the beneficiary to hear. The master trustee may wish to consider these aspects of his recipient: his level of sophistication, education, sense of humor, and learning style, among others.

Separate from the objective issue of the beneficiary's ability to hear is the subjective factor of what he is anticipating. In other words, the master trustee may wish to consider the **Expectations of the Beneficiary**. What, when, and how is he looking to hear?

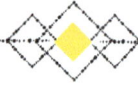

The desired result. This consideration may relate not only to the short-term objectives, but also to long-term objectives of both the trustee and the beneficiary. Further, the goal of one family member may not be the goal of another.

For any communication, there might be multiple and simultaneous purposes which the master trustee should keep in mind. So, for another example, developing a healthy professional relationship with the beneficiary is important and deserving of consideration as a best practice in addition to any specific purpose at hand. This is true because communications are an essential building block of relationship building, along with actions.

The timing of the message. Breakdowns can occur because of the trustee's not recognizing and acting on the difference in the degree of his urgency with that of the beneficiary. So, on the one hand, a trustee may find himself pushing against the resistance of a beneficiary who he perceives to be non-responsive to the trustee's urgency and purpose. Similarly, a trustee may not respond as quickly to a communication for which the beneficiary desires a quick response. It is up to the masterful trustee to minimize the breakdown when encountering either of these known phenomena, and even to leverage them for empowerment.

Consideration of timing and urgency may need to be weighed against the ability of the beneficiary to hear as well as his expectations on how often he could or should be communicating with the trustee. This anticipates the summing up of discretion

in the Action Step of **the context of the communication and its cadence in light of events and other communications**. This choice may be informed by all the above considerations because it is how the discretion manifests itself. The weighing of the elements of discretion may be facilitated by the basic visual aid of a list of pros and cons.

The flow of this interdependency in a real-life example: a young beneficiary refuses the information on the total worth of his trust on his idea that he does not want his actions to be colored by the amount of his inheritance. This boundary wall exists in tension with the trust's specific provisions that provide for the distribution of a percentage of the corpus to him over time, as well as to the trustee's general duties to report what is as to the status of the assets, and how they may have been spent over time. This situation may be satisfactorily leveraged by an agreement over who will review the information (for example, the trust protector or the beneficiary's mother) as well as the trustee warning the beneficiary as to communications which attach the unwelcomed data. Further, the trustee might develop a strategy for expanding over time the beneficiary's ability and willingness to receive this information, which may be part of a financial empowerment goal of the trust.

Hopefully, I've succeeded in sketching out some key communication considerations, and how Polarity Thinking can be an aid. Let's conclude our examination of key polarities in the trustscape with a return to the core value of loyalty.

More on the Duality of the Trustee's Loyalty and the Practices Flowing from Them.

Returning to the practices and tools presented earlier, all of them either form interdependent pairs with each other or are embedded in other polarities – or both.

We've expressly set out and mapped one duality inherent in considering the ultimate trustee value of loyalty, consisting of his need to address the interdependent pair of the trust creator's wishes AND the needs of the beneficiary.

Further study reveals an interdependency in consideration of the actual *actions* of the trustee to be loyal and the *perceptions* of those actions by the beneficiary. In other words, does the beneficiary perceive the actions of the trustee as demonstrating loyalty? Failure to at least manage this interdependent pair may well have contributed to the breakdown underlying the claims of the beneficiaries against the trustee in the *Spencer v. DiCola* lawsuit.

Another often-overlooked interdependency around the trustee's loyalty can consist of the poles of

- the trustee's loyalty to the trust principal, whether trust creator or beneficiary,

- the trustee's loyalty to the values and standards of being a trustee,[19]

- the trustee's loyalty to himself, and

- the trustee's loyalty to the law.

For simplicity, we will Polarity Map® this as the trustee's focus on loyalty to himself (of which his professional and legal standards are a part) AND focus on loyalty to his principal.[20] See Image E.

While this Polarity Map® should be self-explanatory, one note is in order. This is to acknowledge that there is a risk management component that appears with both poles. Though my Polarity Map® suggests that "due regard to risk" is a value for the trustee to assess both for himself and his principal, I don't equate the risks and I don't think they should be assessed in the same way.

---

19 This category could also include the values and standards of a master and a member of the Noble Professions. Though not a specific member of any of the four professions that classically comprise the Noble Professions, I would submit the trustee as a modern-day member of this critical and troubled tribe.

20 I address some considerations of loyalty and the law in a separate chapter.

Trustee Loyalty: to himself and to his principal Polarity Map®

Action Steps

How will we gain or maintain the positive results from focusing on this left pole? What? Who? By When? Measures?

1. Trustee/Principal create trust purpose/mission/vision/policies/systems, including trustee compensation and other rules of engagement.
2. Trustee works from Trustee's Playbook.
3. Trustee engages in outside reflection, study, and support.

Action Steps

How will we gain or maintain the positive results from focusing on this right pole? What? Who? By When? Measures?

1. Trustee/Principal create trust purpose/mission/vision/policies/systems, including trustee compensation and other rules of engagement.
2. Trustee works from Trustee's Playbook.
3. Principal engages in outside reflection, study, and support.

Greater Purpose-GPS®
Healthy Trust and Family
Why leverage polarity?

Values = positive results from focusing on the left pole

- Sustainable for trustee: energetically and monetarily.
- True to trustee's values, knowledge, and experience.
- Enhancing trustee's learning and expertise.
- Due regard to trustee's professional risk.

Values = positive results from focusing on the right pole

- Helpful and empowering to principal.
- Taking care of principal's real and perceived needs.
- Enhancing principal's learning and effectiveness.
- Due regard to risks to and for principal.

Trustee Focus AND **Principal Focus**

Early Warnings***

Measurable indicators (things you can count) that will let you know that you are getting into the downside of this left pole.

A. Principal's complaints.
B. Trustee indifference and objectification of the principal.
C. Principal's lack of growth.

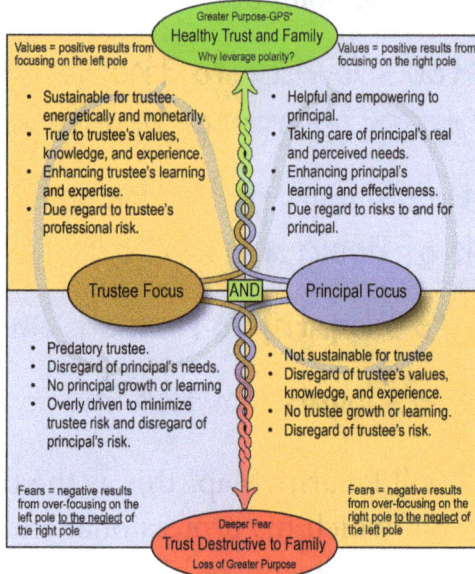

- Predatory trustee.
- Disregard of principal's needs.
- No principal growth or learning.
- Overly driven to minimize trustee risk and disregard of principal's risk.

- Not sustainable for trustee
- Disregard of trustee's values, knowledge, and experience.
- No trustee growth or learning.
- Disregard of trustee's risk.

Early Warnings

Measurable indicators (things you can count) that will let you know that you are getting into the downside of this right pole.

A. Trustee compromised values.
B. Trustee lack of growth.

Fears = negative results from over-focusing on the left pole to the neglect of the right pole

Fears = negative results from over-focusing on the right pole to the neglect of the left pole

Deeper Fear
Trust Destructive to Family
Loss of Greater Purpose

Polarity Map © 1992, 2008 Polarity Partnerships, LLC
Map Content © 2015, 2024 Felix Group, P.C.

Image E. *This Polarity Map® identifies the two poles in the ovals as the polarity of Trustee AND Principal focus to achieve the Greater Purpose of achieving both a healthy trust and family.*

The trustee's primary risk is of being fired, or worse (for both him and for the trust and its stakeholders) being sued. The former, though undesired, may be appropriate if there is no longer a fit between the trustee and the trust stakeholders. The latter is admittedly less desired and can be more unpleasant, again not just for the trustee, but also for the trust and the stakeholders. Claims are not only averse to the trustee but also tend to divert energy and resources away from primary positive trust activities of honoring the trustee and empowering the beneficiaries.

Imagine, for one example, the impact on the Spencer family of enduring a trial and two appeals, all three costly in time and money and attention. And all unsuccessful.

For these risks to himself and his position, a trustee and the trust can purchase insurance. This purchase can be especially appropriate where one of the purposes of a trust is the shifting of risk from the trust creator and his family to the trustee. Significantly, family members serving as fiduciaries often don't appreciate their exposure to their personal liability, failing to recognize that obtaining insurance may be prudent both for the trust and for themselves.

In addition to purchasing insurance, the trustee may be able to appropriately limit his risk by utilizing Polarity Thinking. First, consider the premise that a trust administered successfully for its stakeholders should also be one in which the trustee is less subject to claims. And so, by helping to establish a successfully functioning trust, Polarity Thinking necessarily provides a shield to risk. Second, a written Polarity Map® may satisfy compliance requirements for documenting the process of his decision-making. For instance, the Map could be offered as evidence in those jurisdictions where the trustee's legal liability hinges more on his documentation of an appropriate process than over his taking the precisely correct action. This is another reinforcement of the process component of the trust administration.

The failure to balance the trustee's risk against the risk of the family leads to a perversity of the corporate or other professional trustee. That is the perversity of the trustee being oversensitive to his own risk and simultaneously under appreciative of the risk to the trust family. In this distorted frame of mind, the trustee can make decisions induced by an undue fear of exposure that are at odds with what's best for the family. In fact, this distortion is a known unintended consequence of professional trust administration. I've seen it too often: family members knock on my door in an effort to escape being subjected to this unfortunate practice by their present trustee.

As to the family's risks, it's well known that the family risks the trust's financial assets that are in the protection of the trustee. In addition to these financial risks, the risk to the family also includes the invaluable intangibles of family harmony as well as individual family member fulfillment and empowerment. The family is vulnerable both as to those members presently in the care of the trustee and to the extent that the present generation is reasonably part of the experience and foundation for future generations.[21] For all these reasons, due regard to the trustee's risk looks very different than due regard to the principal's risk.

Both the Polarity Map® and this risk management issue forms a variation of Buber's interdependent pair of "Self AND Other." The proposed Action Steps are what can help keep the trustee

---

21 For more on what is at risk for the family, see the discussion of the core practice of protection in the section on the business of Trusts and the section with The Trustee's Playbook.

focused on his principal as a person and not an "it." The master trustee should also be mindful generally of the oscillation in his intentions and actions between I-It and I-Thou relationships with his families. This is a subject we'll visit more in the next chapter on the Five Energies.

Moving from a direct consideration of loyalty to the trustee's six core practices which flow from loyalty, let's deepen our discussion through the lens of Polarity Thinking. In addition to further understanding and manifesting loyalty, adopting the Polarity Thinking lens facilitates all six of the essential practices of the trustee.

Let's remind ourselves of that list.

- Establish "What Is"
- DO What's Best
- Protect "What Is"
- Communicate
- Build Trust
- Foster growth

Each of these trustee practices benefit from the lens of Polarity Thinking.[22]

---

22 We'll discuss the six practices in greater depth in Section five, The Trustee's Playbook.

First, the practice of *defining* "what is" is interdependent with *creating* "what is." This pair echoes the known universal interdependency of Continuity AND Change.

Second, time and resources necessarily limit each of the six practices. This tension may be expressed by the known interdependency of "Breadth AND Depth."

Further, I've suggested that a system of best practices pairs several of the six core practices into independency. Therefore, "Establishing What Is" enjoys a similar relationship with "doing what's best." Making a memo of What Is without acting on it may provide evidence to a prosecuting litigator embarrassing to the trustee. On the other hand, trying to do what's best without establishing "what is" may be likened to asking the doctor for a prescription without first letting him examine the patient. This echoes the known interdependency of "Plan AND Execute."

Our system of six core practices also pairs communication with both the best practices of "establishing what is" and "doing what's best." This echoes the known interdependency of "Task AND Relationship" – relationship being primarily accomplished through communication. A trustee who focuses on the Task without due appreciation of his relationship with the stakeholders may be engaging in unsustainable activity because it may lead to a poor relationship, and deterioration of trust despite the trustee otherwise doing the right thing. See again the discussion of the *Spencer v. DiCola* case. On the other hand, focusing on

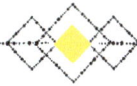

his relationship with the beneficiary (or with the trust creator) without performing the core trustee tasks may lead the trustee to violate his responsibilities.

Acknowledging the embedded interdependency, as discussed above, effective communication necessitates the consideration of the interdependency of the additional practices of exercising honesty/transparency AND exercising prudence/discretion. In addition to "Intention AND Impact," two other known polarities are embedded in communications: "Challenge AND Support" as well as "Advocate AND Inquire."

The core practice of building trust, relying in heavy part on communication, implicates the same interdependent pairs.

The core practice of fostering growth entails the known interdependency of "Lead AND Empower."

The trustee's execution of all six of the core practices entails leveraging the known polarities of "Visionary AND Grounded" as well as "Structured AND Flexible" and also "Advocate AND Inquire."

On a higher level, it should also be seen how these six core trustee practices interrelate with each other as a set of multarities, that is, more than two interdependencies. The master trustee leverages in the moment, engaging in Establishing AND Doing AND Protecting AND Communicating AND Building Trust AND Fostering Growth.

In addition to these polarities embedded and otherwise implicated in the Six Core practices, there are polarities in our list of the dozen additional practices. Let us remind ourself of that list now.

- *Commit to excellence*

- *Cultivate technical knowledge*

- *Cultivate Intelligences*

- *Cultivate being wholly present and mindful*

- *Be Meticulous*

- *Consider the Big Picture*

- *Deliver Results*

- *Honor Process*

- *Be honest and transparent*

- *Exercise prudence and discretion*

- *Be responsive*

- *Set boundaries and limits (cultivate efficiency)*

Those involved in the first four of the twelve may not be as obvious as those in the last eight, which I've set out in pairs.

In committing to Excellence, a master trustee must recognize that sometimes he will have to act with what he considers to be

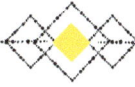

insufficient knowledge. This invokes the known interdependency of "Plan AND Execute." Further, the excellence of any task can be measured not just against his intention, but also how it is perceived. The universal interdependency of "Intention AND Impact" is necessarily again involved.

Finally, and perhaps most significantly, the value pair for excellence may be expressed as "valuing doing" and also "learning from mistakes." Expressing only the value of Excellence is a set up for impossible standards. In contrast, considering the value of Excellence with its interdependent pair of learning from mistakes, the trustee and the trust is put in a position of strength. As one example, I acknowledge that because I am a human, I will sometimes render imperfect results as trustee and so that in addition to making good, I will make it a learning experience for me as well as for other interested stakeholders. The master trustee should have some practice to deal with what will inevitably go wrong.

These polarities involved in the best practice of Committing to Excellence are virtually identical to those involved in both the best practices of "Cultivating Technical Knowledge AND Cultivating Intelligences." The master trustee should consider the interdependencies of both "Plan AND Execute" and also "Intention AND Impact," as well as "Excellence AND Learning."

In contrast, the interdependency for the trustee to consider when dealing with the fourth best practice of being wholly

present and mindful is implied from the word "present." The present is in a dynamic tension with both the past and the future. While staying with what is going on in the present is essential, without additionally considering a vision for the future and an understanding of the past, it may be aimless or worse. Under the lens of Polarity Thinking, a trustee can consider time in various groupings, such as "Past AND Present" or "Past AND Future," and together in the multarity of "Past AND Present AND Future."

The 5th and 6th best practice of the dozen form an interdependent pair together. Specifically, being meticulous, and so attentive to detail, is in tension with remaining mindful of the big picture. Success hinges on the execution of both; neither is sufficient on its own. This interdependency echoes the known interdependency of "Part AND Whole," with the counter-intuitive wisdom that only by focusing on *both* the part and the whole can we succeed in taking care of *either* the part or the whole.

Similarly, the next pair of best practices, namely, Delivering Results and Honoring Process, also form an interdependent pair. Results achieved indifferent to process may be less appreciated and may even provoke unrest or even claims for the violation of the procedures. On the other hand, process not supporting an achievement may result in dissatisfaction for not accomplishing anything.

We've already discussed – and even mapped – the next pair from our list, "Transparency AND Discretion," acts in the guise of "Secured AND Shared Communications."

Finally, the last two practices – "Being Responsive/Available AND Setting Boundaries/Limits" – also form an interdependent pair. This pair echoes the known interdependency of "Activity AND Rest."

Having sketched out many of the key polarities in a trustee's loyalty, let's consider a few more interdependent pairs which a trustee may likely encounter.

A Few other Noteworthy Polarities in the Trustscape.

Beyond the polarities implicated in my list of best practices above, there are additional polarities worthy of note. First, the Intergenerational Oscillation identified by Schuman and her team refers to the known phenomena of the pendulum swinging back and forth over the generations. For one example, a generation of entrepreneurs may be followed by a generation of creative types, philanthropists, and those who have skills and focus seemingly opposite to the entrepreneurial. In mapping the generational difference, the family may also appreciate the greater tapestry of the family over multiple generations as well as the challenges that each individual encounters on their respective journeys, often requiring extensive focus on the family member occupying an extreme part of the system, also known as the Black Sheep.

Spiral Dynamics can be helpful in supporting the journeys of both the individual and the family through Intergenerational

Oscillation. The description of those journeys by Dr. Clare Graves, a thought leader of Spiral Dynamics, resonates with Polarity Thinking: "an emergent, oscillating, spiraling process marked by progressive subordination of older, lower-order behavior systems to newer, higher-order systems as…. existential problems change." These lower-order behavior systems don't disappear under Spiral Dynamics theory, but instead are incorporated into the higher-order system. This helpful concept is reflected in the Polarity Thinker's insistence that parts of reality don't disappear, and so must be incorporated with a healthier restructuring of the system.

This intergenerational divergence in the family can also appear in families as the interdependent pair of "Doing AND Being" as well as "Masculine AND Feminine energy." The latter, having nothing to do with the actual gender of the family members, is a key interdependency. In fact, the impact of multiple breakdowns is compounded when all the stakeholders align with masculine energy.

Mapping this intergenerational oscillation can be a helpful exercise while simultaneously mapping other polarities in a particular trust. At its holy best, mapping this swing of the generations can lead to greater respect for the older generations while also providing greater affirmation for both the differences and similarities of the present and future, as well as offer a map forward.

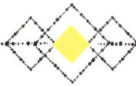

Another prominent set of interdependent pairs in the trustscape is "Structure AND Culture," to which Image F offers a Polarity Map® representing key aspects of the relationship.

Structure AND Culture Polarity Map®

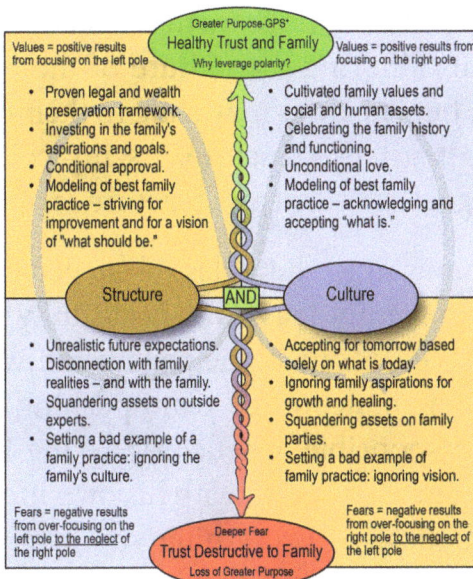

Action Steps
How will we gain or maintain the positive results from focusing on this left pole? What? Who? By When? Measures?

Family/Trustee create:

1. Trust purpose/mission/vision statement.
2. Stewardship, governance policies, procedures, and budgets.
3. Communication process and systems.
4. Change methodologies.

Greater Purpose-GPS*
Healthy Trust and Family
Why leverage polarity?

Values = positive results from focusing on the left pole

- Proven legal and wealth preservation framework.
- Investing in the family's aspirations and goals.
- Conditional approval.
- Modeling of best family practice – striving for improvement and for a vision of "what should be."

Values = positive results from focusing on the right pole

- Cultivated family values and social and human assets.
- Celebrating the family history and functioning.
- Unconditional love.
- Modeling of best family practice – acknowledging and accepting "what is."

Action Steps
How will we gain or maintain the positive results from focusing on this right pole? What? Who? By When? Measures?

Family/Trustee:

1. Conduct inventories and assessments.
2. Celebrate "what is."
3. Monitor impact of structures.
4. Adopt communication process and system.

Structure AND **Culture**

Early Warnings*
Measurable indicators (things you can count) that will let you know that you are getting into the downside of this left pole.

A. Lack of progress around vision and goals.
B. Unaddressed or unresolved family complaints or concerns.
C. Addiction and other dysfunction.
D. No "buy-in."
E. Trustee/family communications changing so quickly, member participation is lost.

- Unrealistic future expectations.
- Disconnection with family realities – and with the family.
- Squandering assets on outside experts.
- Setting a bad example of a family practice: ignoring the family's culture.

- Accepting for tomorrow based solely on what is today.
- Ignoring family aspirations for growth and healing.
- Squandering assets on family parties.
- Setting a bad example of family practice: ignoring vision.

Early Warnings
Measurable indicators (things you can count) that will let you know that you are getting into the downside of this right pole.

A. Absence of family vision and goals.
B. Absence of discipline and work.
C. No evolution in trustee/family communications.

Fears = negative results from over-focusing on the left pole to the neglect of the right pole

Deeper Fear
Trust Destructive to Family
Loss of Greater Purpose

Fears = negative results from over-focusing on the right pole to the neglect of the left pole

Polarity Map © 1992, 2008 Polarity Partnerships, LLC
Map Content © 2015, 2024 Felix Group, P.C.

Image F. *This Polarity Map® identifies the two poles in the ovals as the polarity of Structure AND Culture to achieve the Greater Purpose of achieving both a healthy trust and family.*

To attempt to set up a system of governance or any rules over a family is doomed to failure without due consideration of the culture of the family. Similarly, the focus of a family's culture without a healthy regard for appropriate structure is an

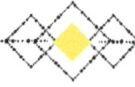

invitation to self-indulgence. One place the breakdown of the due management of this interdependent pair appears is in the troubled dynamics between what the trustee attempts to establish through his understanding of the trust (structure) without those actions being informed by a healthy *kavanah* around the beneficiaries and their world (culture). The more the trustee pushes to establish structure without honoring the culture of the beneficiaries, the more fiercely the beneficiaries may cling to their culture and push back against the trustee's structure. As my colleague Matthew Wesley's truism goes, culture eats structure for breakfast.

This degeneration around the poles of "structure AND culture" in the setting of a family trust was beautifully captured in the movie Citizen Kane. In one scene we see the well-aged banker trustee, who has spent scores of years pushing Kane to live up to his ideal of a responsible beneficiary, asking Kane what Kane otherwise wanted to accomplish with his own life. Kane responds simply and dramatically, "Everything you hate." It's no accident that in the scene Kane has difficulty speaking directly to his trustee, and needs the intermediation of his assistant, Bernstein.

The movie shows well how the trustee is complicit with Kane's parents in depriving him of love and of boundaries. Kane's fatal flaw flows from being unable to overcome this primal loss. The trustee's lack of sensitivity furthers the degeneration of Kane's situation and of the energy within his various polarities, including "Structure AND Culture." Throughout, the trustee slides

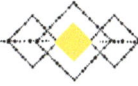

righteously from optimism to exasperation that Kane is a *bad* beneficiary. This degeneration is textbook for Polarity Thinkers around Structure AND Culture.

A related set of interdependent pairs is identified by Schuman and her colleagues as "Tradition AND Change." This is the same interdependency considered by Collins in his book *Good to Great*. Collins calls it "preserve the core and stimulate progress." It can be positively expressed as: how do we keep the best of the past while adopting necessary innovation? This interdependency is also related to intergenerational oscillation, and may appear in families in various related forms, such as "tradition AND freedom," "stability AND creativity," "opened AND closed," or "appreciation AND improvement or repair," among other possibilities. It should be worthwhile for the master trustee involved in administering a trust for a family over a significant enough period of time to leverage this interdependency.

Finally returning to the first of the three perspectives for trustee mastery, *kavanah*, the trustee's higher set of intentions for the family enjoys an interdependent partner or two. One partner is seen within the range of types of intentions that a person can bring. This can be a spiritual intention as well as strategic and physical. One is not better than the other in this Interdependency analysis. In fact, we need to leverage both higher and lower intentions to be in our mastery game.

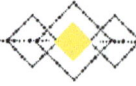

Another partner to *kavanah* is the idea of *keva*, the state of being fixed, stable, or permanent. The valence here is that while *kavanah* is soulful spirit, *keva* is dependable physicality. This duality can also be expressed as that of "thought AND action." Thinking good thoughts doesn't automatically translate into good action or to actions that are appreciated by beneficiaries as good.[23] Therefore, our approach towards mastery is characterized by both an "Intention AND Action."

The Practice of Polarity Thinking in the Trustscape.

Hopefully, by now you appreciate how Polarity Thinking is a helpful tool for the trustee to help the family. In the hands of a master, Polarity Thinking can aid in the leveraging of the assets of the family in deep and significant ways. Another way of saying it: the trustee's exercise of Practical Wisdom is facilitated by Polarity Thinking.

The choice and leveraging of competing values are what Polarity Thinking details. Using a Polarity lens builds competence in Practical Wisdom by revealing the interdependent pairs embedded in that competition and how to leverage them. A masterful trustee will create and leverage Polarity Thinking as appropriate to deal with the situation at hand for – and sometimes with – the various stakeholders of the trust. The specifics of the situation are the driver, which may in some instances call for mapping an interdependency.

---

23 Abraham Joshua Heschel expressly labeled this duality of kavanah and keva as a "polarity."

Given that the competing elements are inherent and not going away, the trustee may revisit these Polarity Maps® periodically as part of best practices. He may perform this practice by himself and, as the situation suggests, with the stakeholders. In fact, the stakeholders may even take on some parts of mapping on their own. In addition to being documented in detail, Polarity Maps® can also be sketched out on the fly, as needed. In fact, with time and experience, a trustee can incorporate mapping into his consciousness and create Polarity Maps® intuitively.

More squarely applying Polarity Thinking to family meeting practices, a family can actually stand in each of the quadrants of the specific interdependency under consideration. So, you can sketch a Polarity Map® on the floor and then walk with the family through the Polarity Map,® physically standing and taking on the experience of intergenerational oscillation, the upside of each of those energies and then the downside. This can be a helpful, and sometimes even transformational, experience.

As an example, let's return to Tom and Betty.

Tom first understands that he's dealing with an interdependency — the core interdependency of the trustscape. This means there's a process of considering the elements of the interdependent pair, and it's not a simple decision, even in the possible but unlikely event that the language of the trust leaves no room for discussion.

Empowered with his version of the "Gifting and Receiving" Polarity Map,® Tom can look at the whole of the system, and not just a part. He must look to his responsibilities to empower and benefit Betty as well as his responsibilities to carry out the directions of Calvin, the trust creator.

He can use the Polarity Map® to organize the many facts which we're not privy to, such as among others, the language of the trust including whether Calvin expressly defined education to exclude her intuition classes, and to what extent Tom retains discretion or is able to rely on another distribution provision to fund Betty's training.

Especially if his decision does not favor Betty, Tom may find it appropriate and helpful to walk Betty through the Polarity Map® to demonstrate his analysis as well as to demonstrate the importance to him of benefitting her in other ways and perhaps even of her involvement and opinion. This may mitigate her disappointment and preserve or even enhance her confidence and trust in Tom – or not.

Though individuals and situations will vary from trust to trust, the trustee who applies and leverages Polarity Thinking may better help his trust families deal with and positively leverage the inescapable features of their experience, including their trust.

Chapter Eleven
The Five Energies

A nother lens of importance for the master trustee acknowledges five energies, representing the multi-dimensionality of reality. The sources for the five energies resonate in ancient wisdom of the Buddha[24] and appear deeply and mystically in the Tanya,[25] which is the founding document of Chasidic Judaism. Kathy Brown is a secular practitioner, who divined the five energies without having been versed in any of the ancient wisdom. She created and teaches the SIPPE™ system, and also consults on trusts.

Simply put, the five energies are identified by the SIPPE acronym:

Spiritual, *which is visionary as well as universal.*

Intellectual, *which is strategic as well as cerebral.*

Physical, which is the concrete, visible, and tangible.

Psychological, *which covers all relations both within and outside of self.*

Emotional, *which is a Geiger counter revealing the pathway as well as the intensity of an experience. In this role, the Emotional is a strong link to "what is." Further, the emotions from fun and play are the more desirable supports for learning and growth.*

---

24 The Buddhist concept of the five languages overlaps with that of the five energies. See, for example, Thich Nhat Hanh.

25 The Tanya contains the ideas and teachings of the founder of the Chabad movement, Rabbi Schneur Zalman (~1745-1812). His articulation of the five worlds overlaps that of the Five Energies. The SIPPE names are almost exactly mapped to the five worlds in the more secular and accessible interpretation of the Tanya by Rabbi Rami Shapiro: "The literal translation of these five dimensions are action, formation, creation, emanation, and primordial human, but from the human perspective, they are better understood as physical, emotional, intellectual, social, and spiritual."

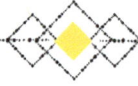

Ultimately, enlightenment or true euphoria is obtained through our unique expression of the human spirit, through the merging of all five energies while simultaneously maintaining each of their individual characters. And in this way, managing and leveraging the Five Energies as a multarity calls on Polarity Thinking skills.

The Five Energies further expand to another level. Each energy may be subdivided or accessed by the other four. For example, this book's expression in words employs primarily intellectual energy to consider all the energies. Alternatives would be to consider the energies from one of the other energies, such as through meditation, dance, music, or face-to-face. This is summed up by the old saw that *talking* about something, such as spirituality, is different than *doing* spiritual or *being* spiritual. Recognition and application of these Five Energies can be useful to the trustee, and those interested in the issues of the trustscape in various ways.

We should first recognize the implication of the five energies in terms of Polarity Thinking. The system of the energies consists of five poles, or more simply, a multarity of five. All of the energies are essential. None of the Five Energies is sufficient on their own. Further, relying on one energy to the exclusion of others leads to a less than ideal, if not a negative result from the imbalance.

Next, applying *kavanah*. The energies work best when there is a harmony of all of them, that is, when there is an oscillation in

the positive realm, weaving in and out to support the whole.[26] To best leverage the energies, Brown suggests constructing a virtual roundtable staffed by personification of the five energies. This technique takes to the next level the mere identification of each energy's upside and downside, but to give them voice in an ongoing discussion.

Like Polarity Thinking, the perspective of the Five Energies recognizes a dynamic system – not just because of the constancy of change, but also because change is required for growth. The use of the virtual roundtable and of Polarity Thinking and Polarity Maps® is an aid to leveraging the system of the Five Energies, including to:

- Identify which perspective may be in the lead at a particular junction;

- Decide when and how it is prudent to involve another energy; and

- Transition from one energy to another.

Moving from process issues to substantive considerations, let's first look at "what is" in the trustscape. The distinctions of the Five

---

26 Note how Brown's choice of the word "weaving" expressly echoes that of Tantra wisdom. In fact, the word "tantra" is often translated as "weaving."

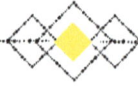

Energies help expose weaknesses in current practices around the creation as well as in the administration of trusts. Knowing the weaknesses, we can improve accordingly.

Typically, a trust is an intellectual approach around finances. Though money and finances invoke various energies, too often in the trustscape money is addressed only as an intellectual and physical aspect of the family's assets. Further, lawyers are stereotypically intellectuals. Their strategies around taxes and legal systems are also intellectual. Similarly, the laws which regulate and form the outside boundaries of the trust are intellectual constructs which also do not relate expressly to the spiritual, psychological, or emotional realities of any given family. *The trust is ultimately an intellectual design of a physical system – with the trustee as the keeper of dollars handed to the beneficiaries at certain times.*

The imbalance caused by this primarily intellectual approach is magnified because of a further distinction that the intellectual platform in which we analyze can be accessed through at least two different frequencies. Simply put, the intellectual mind can either be a "higher" or a "lower" mind. The limitation of the lower intellectual mind is that it is created only from what is already proven in the rational realm. In contrast, the higher intellectual mind – one that embraces *kavanah* – is shaped by the big picture, where we can access endless possibilities.

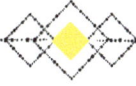

The dynamic of higher and lower mind is another interdependent pair subject to the help of Polarity Thinking. Both higher and lower intellectuality are essential, and neither is sufficient on its own. Therefore, as a further deepening of our concept of *kavanah*, Brown recalls the common wisdom that powerful harmony comes from having one foot solidly planted on the ground and the other flying freely in endless possibilities.

Too often intellectual analysis in the trustscape is exercised only at a lower mind perspective. The limitations imposed by a lower intellectualism without due regard to the higher often manifest as nightmare. One manifestation of the nightmare is that of the "competent" older sibling named as trustee for the "not quite financially making it" younger sibling. Applying the incomplete logic of lower intellect without holding the higher intellect as well, the older brother trustee sometimes turns into a sanctimonious, legalistic bully, seemingly indifferent to the real needs of his younger brother the beneficiary. This known phenomenon is also hostile to the blossoming of the younger brother.

However, even a full-spectrum intellectual and physical approach is insufficient without due consideration of the other energies, particularly the relational aspect of families as well as the spiritual. As we know from Polarity Thinking, *this is not a call to end intellectual or physical so much as to blend it powerfully with these other energies.*

The way forward in blending the energies in the trustscape is to reconsider the starting point. Though often intellectual energy may be the best way into engagement with the stakeholders, oftentimes a family and its professionals will get further and faster *starting* with a spiritual and relational approach, as opposed to an intellectual approach. Recently Simon Sinek demonstrated this principle with his call to start with the "why."

So-called values-based planning accesses at least some of the spiritual, though often does not connect with much, if any of the relational. The gap in the relational is revealed by the focus on the wealth creator and his wishes and needs, as opposed to also consideration of those of his descendants and his significant other. To the extent these others are considered, it is too often only from his point of view, instead of robustly from theirs. This near-sightedness is exacerbated by the default intellectual structure of having a trust's legalistic administrative governance stand in for independent family decision-making and values.

Another opportunity to apply the Five Energies may be seen in one of the known breakdowns from the solely intellectual approach to planning. Often the estate planner will craft his intellectual solution, but the client will drag his feet or disappear. I submit that the client's reluctance is the failure to connect with his emotional, spiritual, and psychological energies. The vehicle to transport the family through the intergenerational transition could first take into account *who* the family is and the vision of where they are going.

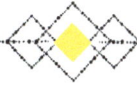

The intellectual approach in estate planning could be in service of those spiritual and relational ideas, rather than trying to shoehorn family considerations into a vehicle that is designed simply to avoid probate and taxes. The Five Energies are a gateway for estate planning to enhance family harmony and to empower families.

Turning more squarely to trust administration, it's often useful for the trustee to utilize all the Five Energies. Typically, the trustee employs solely an intellectual language. Intellectual language is often insufficient on its own, beyond what has already been discussed. First, an intellectual connection is inadequate on its own because of the primarily nonintellectual nature of both family and money. One family dynamics practitioner, Gary Shunk, estimates that at least 80% of any money conversation connects to psychological and emotional aspects. Further, the interpersonal connection between the trustee and a beneficiary may be weakest if relying only on intellectual energy. Indeed, generally the more of the Five Energies that are shared, the stronger any interpersonal connection.

Connecting to the beneficiary on a spiritual level may include the beneficiary's vision for himself and for his family. That vision may be on various levels, such as personal, professional, or financial. It may even include both his cosmology as well as his religious views, though it does not have to. As Brown opines, "A fully developed spiritual energy involves the free flow of information back and forth between the soul and the physical mind and body."

This can only be accomplished by choosing to break through fear. While the beneficiary retains the choice to participate in that discussion or not, the masterful trustee will do his best to facilitate that discussion, including to plant seeds and otherwise create supportive structures.

Connecting to the beneficiary psychologically may include his relationship to himself, to the trustee, to the vision of the trust creator and to the other trust stakeholders, to the money, and to his own family, and to transition plans. There's another level of relationship for members of the same pot trust, as well as members involved in a joint family enterprise.

One way to layer in the spiritual and relational energies is through the creation of written intentions and goals for the trust. The trustee might initiate this project, creating a draft document which incorporates the trust creator's expressions, and the beneficiaries needs and wants along with his own wisdom. He might invite comments or even cocreation with the beneficiary and other stakeholders. The statements of both investment and distribution policy may flow from this project. In their creation, these statements may include the larger vision of spirituality and big mind intellectuality, the relationship of the beneficiary and trust creator, as well as the relationship of the trustee and beneficiary, and the beneficiary with his journey. And, once drafted, these documents may support ongoing and perhaps deepening discussions at the annual meetings.

Connecting to the beneficiary physically often takes some greater creativity and effort. That's because our default communication is typically through the intellectual filter of words, especially through the written word, such as email or text. Ritual can be a good connection physically, as well as on other levels. In its gathering and assembling, a family meeting is physical, as is a one-on-one meeting. Working through the polarities by standing in the various quadrants of the applicable Polarity Map,® can also be a powerful way to connect to the physical.

In a simple and fun exercise, Jay Hughes documents the successful leveraging of physical energy in the practice of having family members wear articles of clothing at a family meeting which identify each of their particular and various cohorts. Jay cites *Hats Off to You* by Lee Hausner and Ernest Doud, Jr. for inspiring him in this practice that involves members of the same generation wearing, say, a particular type of hat, while descendants from a particular family member each wear the same color and style shirt. In so doing, the family makes a representation in physical reality which tends to deepen their connection with the flow of various polarities.

Considerations of the Five Energies in trust administration provides additional support for known best practices. It shouldn't be a surprise that the five energies highlight the importance of the

practice of legacy and philanthropy projects. These projects often work on all five levels, specifically:

> *Spiritually in connecting to a vision larger than oneself.*
>
> *Intellectually in devising strategies and other mental work to accomplish the project.*
>
> *Physically in the performance of various work and the creation of the tangible forms that the legacy may take (a book or video, for example) or in the execution of the philanthropic work.*
>
> *Psychologically in connecting to present and past family members as well as to those involved and served by the project as well as exercising joint-decision making.*
>
> *Emotionally in various ways, such as the deep satisfaction in giving, in experiencing the gift being well-received and in completing the project as well as in working together.*

As another example of best practice, stories can also work on multiple levels, especially when well-crafted to include all Five Energies. The story of an ancestor overcoming hardship may involve all five, especially when the storyteller is sensitized to including the various energies in the listening experience.

Most importantly, the master trustee employs the Five Energies inclusively to more successfully serve his families and honor the kavanah of the trust.

Section Three

Trustee Laws, Their Importance, and Their Limitations

66

Justice H: The law is the will of the Justices.
Justice S: No, law is that which is right.

~ Langbridge's Case, decided 1345

99

I've deliberately avoided discussing trust laws until now. Others seem to overemphasize the importance of these laws. Specifically, some sources maintain that the laws provide the sole guidance for trust administration. While the laws are important, essential even, in determining "What Is" for a trustee, the laws are generally a poor guide to best practices for a trustee.

Chapter Twelve
The Rules and Their Essential Importance

The primary source for the responsibilities of a trustee is the trust document. Yet that document does not exist in a vacuum. Instead, each trust lives on the sea of the rules of a legal jurisdiction. As an example, a trust which is governed by the laws of the State of Illinois, must be interpreted in the context of the laws of Illinois, which include both statutes and decisions of the Illinois courts.

Illinois, like many other jurisdictions, does not permit a trust to do away with certain core duties of a trustee. These duties are basically as follows:

- *Duty of Loyalty and to Avoid Conflicts of Interest and Impartiality*

- *Duty to Administer the Trust by its Terms*

- *Duty To Exercise Skill and Care at a Significant Level*

- *Duty to Communicate, including Notices and Accountings*

- *Duty not to Delegate Certain Tasks*

- *Duty to Keep Trust Property Separate from his Own and Others*

- *Duty to Invest and Preserve Assets, including to Enforce and Defend Claims*

Depending on the duty, the jurisdictions may permit some limitations of the duties, as well as some limitations on the liability

for their breach. For instance, a trust may be permitted to limit the liability of the trustee for intentional or gross violations, and to not hold the trustee responsible for simple mistakes. This would be an appropriate limitation to an uninsured family member trustee, among others.

The duties are officially interpreted by the courts of the various jurisdictions and are also discussed on a national if not international basis through various uniform codes. There is considerable literature on these duties, including through the ongoing court decisions ruling on alleged violations.

The essentials of these duties are expressed as *minimums*. In other words, the exercise embodied in these duties, and their application is to determine what is the minimum necessary for the trustee to not breach a duty. As one key example, the duty in a jurisdiction may be to supply the beneficiary with a minimum of one accounting per year. A trustee who does not provide an accounting once a year is then likely breaching his legal duty if he does not provide an accounting each year. In contrast, depending on the situation, the best practice may be to keep the beneficiary informed in real time of the status of his financial accounts.

As another example, I'm unaware of a court expanding on the Duty of Loyalty as we have here. Again, the court is considered in *minimums*, we're concerned with best practices. The prudent and masterful trustee will be mindful of these duties, though best practices may hopefully put the trustee at a safe distance from the brink of violation. This is a subject worthy of further explanation.

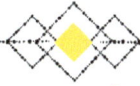

Chapter Thirteen
The Rules are Not the Game

One of the noteworthy paintings of the famous surrealist painter Rene Magritte is called *The Treachery of Images*. This painting reveals a tobacco pipe. Magritte includes a large-type caption "*ceci n'est pas une pipe,*" which translates to "This is not a pipe."

At first glance the graphic is at odds with the caption. Clearly the graphic is a pipe. How can this be something other than a pipe? In keeping with the painting's title, the resolution of the seeming paradox is that Magritte has provided a PICTURE of a pipe. And, of course, a picture which is made of canvas and paint, is not a pipe, which is made from wood.

The treachery revealed by this example is that an image can be mistaken for the real thing. In the same fashion, successful trust administration has often been conflated and confused with the minimums which the trust laws establish.

Consider another example: the rules of baseball adopted by the Major Leagues of the United States. Baseball rules provide for the fundamentals, such as that first base shall be 90 feet from home base. The rules also provide for more esoteric situations such as the procedures around a ball hit as an Infield Fly. As essential as the rules of baseball are to the game, it's a safe call to assume that the winning baseball teams are NOT studying those rules on game day. Although they still need to know the rules, such as the details of handling an infield fly, those rules are far from enough. The winning team is studying their playbook, observing

the strengths and weaknesses of the opposing team and the like. It's this study and practice around their playbook which will lead them to success on game day.

In short, knowing the rules of baseball does not make one a good baseball player. Instead, knowing and practicing the strategies of winning baseball is the road to a team's success.

In like manner, studying the duties of the trustee under the law will not lead to a successful trust. At best, it may well help *avoid* an *un*successful trust. That is, help to avoid the crisis following a violation of certain legal rules.

Significantly, the rules of baseball expressly define success on the diamond: "The objective of each team is to win by scoring more runs than the opponent." In marked contrast, the trust laws do not attempt to define what constitutes a successful trust. Further, *these laws typically don't even acknowledge that there is such a thing as a "successful trust."*

The good news is that the trust laws do NOT stop a trustee from helping to define the purpose of the trust, or to articulate what at any given time are the goals or measures of success of the trust. And the trustee is usually at liberty to help develop the playbook. One playbook is offered in Section five of this book.

Chapter Fourteen
The Minimum is not Necessarily Success

The treachery of trust laws is the implication that not running afoul of those rules constitutes successful trust administration.

This is the same foolishness which would declare that a successful journey in the car is one in which the driver received no traffic tickets. While for some of us drivers, staying ticket-free would be noteworthy, most of us would look to other metrics to define the success of this simple task: did we arrive at our intended destination efficiently and timely with a minimum of stress – or even, was this a good experience?

The questions around meeting the outside boundaries of the law are typically different than the questions around best practices. For example, it's one thing to inquire, "What's the minimum accounting a trustee needs to provide to his beneficiary?" It's quite another to ask, "What's the most prudent, helpful, or empowering access to the accounting information a trustee can provide this particular beneficiary?" The former seeks to simply avoid running afoul; the latter is looking to see what may best serve the beneficiary.

Further, trust administration that focuses on the one will likely be experienced differently by the trust's stakeholders than if the focus is on the other. Would you rather be the recipient of the minimum or of that which will help you grow? Or, perhaps better, would you rather be on a ship captained in a way that is in a game of brinksmanship, or one run smoothly, flowing in an enjoyable journey?

A final example should be helpful. This is to revisit from the court files of trust litigation, the case of Spencer v. DiCola. In this case, the Spencer family alleged various wrongdoing against trustee DiCola, including, among other things, her failure to follow the terms of the trust in approving certain educational expenses. Though the family had earlier selected DiCola to be their trust's administrator, they were seeking her removal in the lawsuit. The court ultimately rejected the family's argument and sustained DiCola as trustee, holding that DiCola had acted consistently with the trust and trust rules.

What the court did not address is the *quality* of DiCola's trust administration. The court did not discuss how the trustee or anyone else defined successful or purposeful distributions, how the trust and the family might be better off if the trustee did in fact resign, even though she wasn't legally obligated to do so, or how this crisis of litigation may impact the future smooth functioning of the trust, or how the trustee served the Spencer family. The court did not discuss these things, because it was legally irrelevant to the court. These questions, however, may have been important for the family – and at least aspirational for a trustee on the journey to mastery.

The court's vindication of the trustee does *not* equate with a finding that this trust was successful or that the family was receiving excellent trust administration.

Chapter Fifteen
It's About What is Right

There's an art and science as to how a trustee might want to establish what is best. I offer my views of that elsewhere in the text. Also, what is best may conflict with law. Given the tender cargo of families and their individual members, it may be possible that in certain, rare situations a trustee may best exercise his duty of loyalty by violating some other trust rule. If this difficult situation should occur, it may be best left to the trustee's conscience and the trust's legal counsel.

Section Four

The Business of the Trustee's Practice

> " *The spirit is a countervailing system, not because it works against success in the world but because it leads the individual away from the fear and desire that require worldly success and toward sufficiency as a state of being.*
>
> ~ **Peter White, Ecology of Being** "

Whether the trustee is being directly paid for his services or not, his work needs to be sustainable. Hopefully, the ideas expressed in the other Sections outline what it takes for the trustee's practice to provide intellectual and spiritual sufficiency. They should also help with social sustenance, both in providing a platform for interactions with family as well as in the collegiality of fellow travelers.

Physical sufficiency includes healthy practices for the trustee's body. Loyalty inspires the trustee to take good care of his body, so it may function well and long in service.

Economic sufficiency works primarily on the physical. It is an essential part of a tangible exchange of providing service. And, at the same time, sufficiency of money to a trustee can be reinforcing and affirming. It can be an expression of love.

Chapter Sixteen
Family Members and Friends

My observation of the present culture is that families generally expect their members to serve as fiduciaries without payment. Like the biblical patriarchs, it's just something that is assumed that the next generation will do.

A family should decide if and how to compensate other family members for serving as trustee as well as for caretaker, in the context of creating the overall transition. The failure of families to do so has led not only to family fractures, but also to legislation which fills the gap to compensate family member caretakers.[27]

Also note the impact of the degree of family readiness for the transition. At one end of the spectrum are those successful so-called multi-generational families, who enjoy a culture that actively engages in generatively preparing for and accomplishing intergenerational transition. The burden of the preparatory work of the trustee may be taken up by the culture: desires, needs, and implementation are, and should be, a real part of the family dialogue and activities.

The active work of the trustee in such a successful multi-generational family may be minimized by this advance work, and further mitigated by the work of other fiduciaries. These others may meet as a family council, may be teaching the next generation how to perform the trustee tasks, and may be instilling the ethos

---

27 In Illinois, a person who dedicates themselves to the care of a disabled family member and who lives with them for at least three years with them may recover directly from the estate, outside of the will and trust. 755 ILCS 5/18-1.1

of trust administration being simply another of the reasonable expectations placed on family members.

Update: I should acknowledge the question of whether a family member trustee can comply with the Duty of Impartiality. The supposition is that training and experience may not be able to overcome deeply set family dynamics. This question was posed by Peter Karoff and continues according to Jay, perhaps particularly when the relationship of trustee to beneficiary is one of parent and child or, in my experience, siblings. Hopefully a well-trained and mindful family member would seek support and pursue options as may be appropriate, such as the appointment of a special trustee for certain specific tasks. I would expect the trust would assume the cost of helping the family member trustee succeed.

Chapter Seventeen
Professionals and the Application of the Six Core Practices

My understanding[28] is that currently most corporate trustee professionals work off of a fee schedule, often based on the amount of assets under management of the trustee. Individual fiduciaries may be paid hourly. I presume I'm not the only trustee offering as an occasional alternative to hourly fees, project fees, flat annual fees and, in certain select situations, success fees.[29]

And of course, the Six Core Practices still apply.

Establish "What Is." Establishing the fee structure is an activity for the present that also may be inspected later in hindsight. Another way to say this is, the trustee must show value in a form that is appreciated.

Do What's Best. Again, "best" is a multi-tiered consideration: the trust creator, the beneficiaries, and other stakeholders may enter into the mix. The question to answer may be: "To the extent

---

28 I am not aware of any survey of trustee compensation, though one would be welcome at least by consumers.

29 Aspects of best practice for success fees may be suggested by the rules governing attorneys for contingency fees. Illinois Professional Responsibility Rule 1.5 (c) provides:

"(c) A fee may be contingent on the outcome of the matter for which the service is rendered, except in a matter in which a contingent fee is prohibited by... law. A contingent fee agreement shall be in a writing signed by the client and shall state the method by which the fee is to be determined, including the percentage or percentages that shall accrue to the lawyer in the event of settlement, trial or appeal; litigation and other expenses to be deducted from the recovery; and whether such expenses are to be deducted before or after the contingent fee is calculated. The agreement must clearly notify the client of any expenses for which the client will be liable whether or not the client is the prevailing party. Upon conclusion of a contingent fee matter, the lawyer shall provide the client with a written statement stating the outcome of the matter and, if there is a recovery, showing the remittance to the client and the method of its determination."

the trustee has flexibility in his fee structure, what fee structure best suits?"

There's also a nice, practical question on whether in this one domain, the trustee may now consider what fees and fee structure works best for him. And even so, the trustee should be concerned if his fee structure is less beneficial or even counter-productive for the stakeholders. Further, are there other trustees whose fee structure is known to be more beneficial?

Doing what's best may include declining a case where the fee structure doesn't work. And here it's worth mentioning the wonderful trustee, who though he declined active service, nevertheless paid for the repair of the electrical system of the home of the prospective client, which he found to be dangerously broken while conducting his due diligence.

There is no requirement or blessing for a trustee to be financially disadvantaged by the relationship, unless deliberately assumed as a *pro bono* project.

Protect "What Is." Protection is a consideration as to how much in fees the trust can support and for how long. For example, a trustee should consider the impact of his fees in deciding whether and when a trust should be terminated. Keeping the trust open merely to keep being paid would be a violation of this practice.

It's worth repeating that to the extent the trustee has flexibility in his fee structure, the trustee should consider what fee structure

best suits. That may even lead to reconsidering the fee structure or amount on a regular basis. My usual practice, as an example, is to reassess the annual fee based on the nature and amount of activity projected for the next year.

Communicate. Communication is a key consideration, and again a multi-tiered one across the levels of those involved: the trust creator, the beneficiaries, and sometimes even some of the other stakeholders. Again, the rules for attorneys are helpful, though the trustee does not have an attorney-client relationship with the other trust stakeholders.[30]

Having the structure in writing is important to maintain clear communication in the moment, and as a record to refer to. The writing can also be essential whereas some services may be extra. Supplementary if not ongoing communications can be helpful when approaching the boundary into those extra fees.

---

30 Illinois Professional Responsibility Rule 1.5 (a) provides:

"(a) A lawyer shall not make an agreement for, charge, or collect an unreasonable fee or an unreasonable amount for expenses. The factors to be considered in determining the reasonableness of a fee include the following:

(1) The time and labor required, the novelty and difficulty of the questions involved, and the skill requisite to perform the legal service properly;

(2) The likelihood, if apparent to the client, that the acceptance of the particular employment will preclude other employment by the lawyer;

(3) The fee customarily charged in the locality for similar legal services;

(4) The amount involved and the results obtained;

(5) The time limitations imposed by the client or by the circumstances;

(6) The nature and length of the professional relationship with the client;

(7) The experience, reputation, and ability of the lawyer or lawyers performing the services; and

(8) Whether the fee is fixed or contingent."

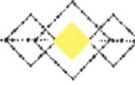

Good communication around billing may suggest monthly statements, which can also serve to inform of the activity of the trustee.

Build Trust. The details of the trustee's compensation as well as how the trustee institutes his compensation will likely build or detract from his trustworthiness. The amount, the communications, and the extent of his protection of the trust all can inform his trustworthiness. As one example, setting expectations as to activity and progress can sometimes be better set by issuing statements regularly rather than one at the end of the year.

Billing structure can impact trust. For example, charging fees through the structure of assets under management may be perceived as disconnected with value or time, or worse, as a structural disincentive to make full and fair distributions. As another example, billing hourly may satisfy some since only being charged for what is consumed, while others prefer not to have a meter running. Hourly billing may be perceived as not related to value, and worse, as a structural incentive to work more.

Extra services may also impact trust. A trustee who is compensated in a separate fee for referrals to other colleagues may not appear to be working for the good of the family as compared to one who is not receiving referral fees.

Foster growth. The trustee's experience with compensation and the families he serves can be a vivid part of his learning. The

trustee can employ his compensation as learning for stakeholders of the trust in a number of ways. The impact on trustee fees of alternative stakeholder actions may be the subject of demonstration and learning.

A specific instance would be over an aging living trust creator's choice as to whether and when to involve a geriatric care manager. To the extent left to the trustee to co-manage in crisis with the holder of the power of attorney for health, the fees could be higher than if the geriatric care manager is hired and gets up to speed in advance of need. I've found families appreciate being given this option.

Another example of providing a laboratory for stakeholder actions would be giving the trust creator of an insurance trust the option to set aside projected annual fees in advance or to simply remain liable as they occur. The trustee can help advise as to the merits of either option, allowing the trust creator to choose. I've found the future experience over that decision to be educational for all involved.

As with other opportunities for learning, the trustee would be well advised to avoid being preachy or otherwise inappropriate.

Chapter Eighteen
Other Thoughts on Fees

*C*onsiderations as to Amount. Those who serve as trustees may be well advised to consider the applicable rules of lawyer professional responsibility as to fees. That's because the relationship of lawyer to client in key respects bears similarity to a trustee's relationship to a trust – even though serving as trustee is neither a job just for lawyers nor is it considered a lawyer-client relationship. In Illinois, there are a number of factors to be considered. Among others, those factors include the difficulty of the assignment as well as the experience, reputation, and ability of the attorney, which may be balanced against the amount involved and the results obtained.[31]

Who needs to agree? Legally, a trustee may not require the signature of anyone over his fees. In some trusts, the trustee's fees may be subject to review by a trust protector or other fiduciary. As a practical matter, the trustee's fees may be a matter of approval of the person who may be selecting or enjoying the services of the trustee: trust creator, beneficiaries, or trusted advisor.

If the fees may come into contention or if the trust is court-supervised, a judge may be asked to review the fees. In the hopes of avoiding contention, the trustee may seek acquiescence, if not consent from the key various stakeholders.

---

31 Illinois Professional Responsibility Rule 1.5 (b) provides:
" (b) The scope of the representation and the basis or rate of the fee and expenses for which the client will be responsible shall be communicated to the client, preferably in writing, before or within a reasonable time after commencing the representation, except when the lawyer will charge a regularly represented client on the same basis or rate. Any changes in the basis or rate of the fee or expenses shall also be communicated to the client."

Section Five
The Trustee's Playbook

> *Always you have been told that work is a curse and labour a misfortune. But I say to you that when you work you fulfill a part of earth's furthest dream, assigned to you when that dream was born, And in keeping yourself with labour you are in truth loving life, And to love life through labour is to be intimate with life's inmost secret.*

~ **Khalil Gibran, *The Prophet***

We've looked deeply at the mindset and practices of a master trustee. I've submitted the idea that the bedrock of the trustee's world is his loyalty. This loyalty is at least dual in nature, including both loyalty to the trust creator and his trust document as well as to the beneficiary. The loyalty to the beneficiary includes consideration of the impact of the trust creator's design, as well as the possibly independent needs and wants of the beneficiary.

In dissecting the concept of a trustee's loyalty, I suggested that from the application of the virtue of Loyalty there flows Six Core Practices and the Dozen Additional Practices. We've looked at all those practices under the three perspectives of *kavanah*, Polarity Thinking, and the Five Energies.[32] I suggested that the master trustee

---

32 In the context of *kavanah* we also mentioned Spiral Dynamics. In the context of Polarity Thinking one can see Spiral Dynamics as a progressive level of systems flowing from the "Part AND Whole" interdependency. The mantra attributed to Ken Wilbur applies here: "Transcend and Include."

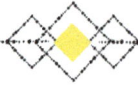

and his administration would benefit from becoming familiar with these practices and perspectives to deepen his ability to work loyally. These various practices and perspectives I refer to collectively as the Trustee's Playbook.

This Trustee's Playbook represents how I aspire to conduct my work as a trustee and can be followed in whole or in part as you determine for your best practices. Either way, it serves as an example of how you can serve your beneficiaries as trustee.

I frame this section around the Six Core Practices that flow from Loyalty. I delve more closely into those situations that a trustee may typically encounter. After considering those six in greater depth, I'll add some overview thoughts. Again, what I am exploring here are best practices; I am not suggesting these as minimum standards.

To refresh, the six core practices are:

- DO What's Best[33]
- Establish "What Is"
- Protect "What Is"
- Communicate
- Build Trust
- Foster growth

---

33 Yes. I've switched the order of the first two Core Practices here for editorial convenience. Thanks for noticing.

Chapter Nineteen
Do What's Best

The other five Core Practices explain what the masterful trustee should be doing to demonstrate loyalty. In contrast, the idea of "Doing What's Best" seems virtually synonymous with the idea of Loyalty, especially when using the lenses of *kavanah*, Polarity Thinking, and the Five Energies.

The Purpose of a Trust Revisited and Distilled.

The trust benefits its beneficiaries according to the wishes of the trust creator. Those wishes would provide the essential understanding as to what this benefit is and how it is to be accomplished. In short, the purpose of a trust is to provide benefit to the beneficiaries.[34] This often, if not typically, appears as providing benefit to the family of the trust creator.[35]

As we know, the trust creator is often the first beneficiary, so in that situation the trust creator intends to receive the benefit from his successor trustee when he can no longer take care of his own affairs. The trust creator and his family may receive other benefits, including certain tax and creditor protection as well as successor and governance provisions, to name just a few of the most frequently cited benefits. Though these expand the existential purpose of taking care of oneself where one cannot otherwise,

---

34 This applies factually and morally even in those jurisdictions, such as Illinois, that have removed this purpose from their trust laws. I do not address so-called beneficiary-less trusts here.

35 I acknowledge and choose not to address in this text the various trusts that don't fit squarely into this typical design.

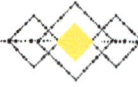

they are all consistent with the principle that the purpose of a trust is to provide a benefit to the beneficiaries.

We can say as a working principle that *the purpose of a trust is to provide a benefit to the trust creator and his family.*

Start with the Trust Documents, but Don't End There.

Given that the trustee is charged with benefiting the trust creator and his family, it follows that the master trustee needs to pay attention to the impact of his administration on these beneficiaries. This is to say, that the trust document is an administration essential, and it's not enough for the masterful trustee to do his job.

This logical inference is supported by our other knowledge and experience.

First, our consideration of the core interdependency in the trustscape demonstrates that the impact of the trust on the beneficiaries is interdependent with honoring the wishes expressed in the trust document. In the real world, the cause of many instances of trust and family breakdown is evidenced by a reliance on the trust document to the exclusion of the impact on the beneficiary.

In my practice, I've identified the Big Brother syndrome.[36] As previously discussed, this syndrome consists of parents naming

---

36 The reference to the dystopian fiction of 1984 by George Orwell is intentional.

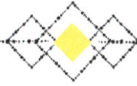

an older son as trustee at their death over a younger son, where the older son has demonstrated some real and practical financial success as compared to the younger's demonstrated weakness in that realm. When the big brother administers his parents' trust, he focuses on the letter of the trust document to the exclusion of consideration of the impact on his younger brother.[37] The result can be extremely painful for the younger brother beneficiary.[38]

This call for the trustee doing his best is also not limited because his role is merely as a financial fiduciary. Money touches everything. Applying the Perspective of the Five Energies and the wisdom of family dynamics, *money is a currency which echoes its sources and uses in the family, as well as the hurts, love, and the imperfections of relationship.*[39] The call to pay attention to the impact of his administration as well as its compliance with the trust document includes considerations of what makes an administration successful.

---

37 Therapists and other counselors have offered insights, including that the big brother adopts this masculine hyperfocus in unconscious defense to a perceived defect in the parents. Consistent with the predictions through Polarity Thinking, if not common sense as well, the more the younger brother resists, often the more entrenched the big brother becomes. Though I've provided various help and relief to the many younger brothers who have walked into my office, I have yet to find an effective invitation to help the big brother become conscious, or to simply embrace the other pole.

38 One such beneficiary reported through tears that he contemplated suicide because of this treatment. Others report feeling infantilized and alienated. The ill effects of this syndrome are not limited to emotions, and include financial loss, increasing indebtedness and professional setbacks.

39 Money as the currency of trusts is worthy of much deeper treatment. Note the various biblical prohibitions of accepting money from certain sources. Compare also, the comment attributed to the Roman emperor Vespasian on the ethics of taxing sewers: *Pecunia non olet* ("money does not stink"). Given the power of money in the trustscape, I suspect Vespasian of wishful thinking.

The charge to the trustee to do his best may be further challenged because successful administration is often not clearly defined in the trust. Is the trustee successful merely because he has distributed the assets as the trust directed? What if he accomplished that asset distribution, but at the price of family harmony – or at the price of demotivating a beneficiary? The masterful trustee will assume responsibility for aiming to accomplish the highest benefit he can: family harmony and empowerment.

This sensitivity of the trustee to Do What Is Best can lead to proactive doing, beyond the scope of the trust documents. Discovering a pot trust shared by two conflicting beneficiaries, he may (as I did) act to decant the trust into two separate trusts so as to separate and ultimately calm the two beneficiaries. In dividing this trust, the trustee may be performing a great benefit to all, which the trust creator (or his attorney) simply did not anticipate.

What Does the Trustee Do?

What the trustee does can be said to depend on the point of view. Consider, for example, this question with the lens of the Five Energies. On an intellectual level, we know that the trustee honors the wishes of the trust creator while empowering the beneficiary. This work is getting from point A to B, however that may be defined in the trust documents and the context.

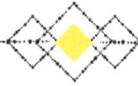

The often-encountered scenarios include…

- *Helping a trust creator through his own disability and then distributing assets on his death.*

- *Guiding a beneficiary through his life.*

- *Mentoring a beneficiary through a period of incompetence (such as legal age).*

- *Ongoing support of a beneficiary with so-called special needs.*

Trustees serving families with great financial wealth or with family businesses may be called in to a variety of additional strategic uses of trusts.

All these intellectual tasks relate to the trust's function as a legal construct. As such, lawyers and accountants duly exploit the trustee's function for efficiency in minimizing taxes and, hopefully also, in maximizing philanthropic impact. However, these professionals often limit their concept of "successful" trust administration to accomplishing these intellectually conceived financial goals.

On a physical level, the trustee is typically engaged in project management, often with two interlocking sets of budgets, one for the current term and the other reflecting longevity of assets, and with interconnected systems for communications, meetings,

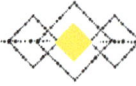

calendar, and information retention. The typical course work addressing "How to Be a Trustee" lives in the physical perspective. Of course, successful completion of these tasks is essential, and, on its own, far from sufficient to achieve masterful administration.

From a psychological point of view, the trustee's work has to do with each beneficiary's relationship to the trust, which includes necessarily the relationship of the beneficiary with the trust creator as well as the beneficiary's relationship with his own self in its many facets, including past, present, and future self. In addition, the trustee must contend with both his and each beneficiary's relationship with the other advisors to the trust. Where there are other trust beneficiaries, the trustee can have the additional challenge of his own as well as each beneficiary's relationship with those other trust beneficiaries. None of these may be simple relationships, given the typical emotional context.

The emotional valence varies, given the often deep personal and familial emotional wellsprings that connect to life, love, loss – and to money. These are typically huge components which are unique to each individual and family, however much there may be common patterns. Family emotions are inextricably involved in the trustee's work – and too often ignored.

Finally, the vision or spiritual task of the trustee is to help to tailor the fabric connecting the rise of one generation to the next. One expression of this generational transition in Judaism is expressed as *l'dor v'dor*, or "from generation to generation." The Hebrew

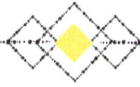

phrase is found in prayer as well as conversation, and refers to a holy continuity, both of individual fulfillment and the flourishing of the tribe. In fact, where the family has not otherwise created culture or structures around their intangible assets of values and legacy, the trustee may be the *only* guardian for these invaluable foundational family assets.

In sum, the trustee's work is described in *all* of these realms simultaneously. In so doing, the trustee's work builds family harmony. In fact, the trustee's strong impact upon family harmony during intergenerational transitions is evidenced empirically by the work of O'Sullivan. Acknowledging the trustee's impact on family harmony necessarily brings the masterful trustee back to loyalty through humility. And in performing the work of loyalty, the trustee on the journey to mastery engages the various loyalty practices we've so far identified.

But again: what does the trustee *do* with this list of practices? How does he decide what to do *now*?

There is a great challenge in deciding in the moment the best action to take. This is the core of application of Practical Wisdom and is answered with the three tools for trustee mastery: *kavanah*, Polarity Thinking, and the Five Energies.

This dilemma is biblical. One example out of the Judeo-Christian bible: God tells Abraham to *listen* to his wife, Sarah, who angrily insists that he banish Hagar and Ishmael. In this account,

Abraham, a consummate doer and pleaser, banishes his loyal servant and their son. Perhaps the course more in tune with family harmony would have been for Abraham to have taken the divine direction more literally and his wife's wish less so, and more on the emotional level, namely, to have *listened* to and consoled Sarah, who was distraught over not having her own child.

President Theodore Roosevelt once said, "Do what you can, with what you have, where you are." This profound truth offers guidance on doing what's best as a trustee. Though critical hindsight is not the thing, neither is shrugging and walking away from a wrong. Repairing the inevitable missteps is another essential of the master trustee's work. My own tools include, where practicable, acknowledging my mistakes, making good and capturing learning for both myself and the trust stakeholders. One could say that the descendants of Isaac and Ishmael are continuing to deal with the repair of the story of Abraham's choices.

The dilemma is existential. Like, Abraham, the trustee has to do *something*. Although that something may be to take counsel and do nothing for the moment.

The special challenges of the trustee's work are the all-too-common low level of preparedness of the family stakeholders as well as the all too typical lack of consensus on what the family goals are, combined with a low degree of cooperation and collaboration amidst elevated emotional turbulence. Consider in marked contrast, the example of the manager of a professional baseball

team who enjoys stakeholders who are typically highly motivated and trained and all focused on winning the World Series.

Doing what's best may lead the trustee to decline assignments that don't fit. Fit, of course, may be assessed in a number of pertinent levels including pricing, geography, or temperament.

Another best practice recommended by Jay Hughes is the trustee standing for regular review. The trustee may be doing what's best by resigning if he is not having a sufficient positive impact in serving the family.

How the Trustee Does it Matters.

How the trustee performs his tasks can be as important as *what* he does. For example, does he distribute money to a beneficiary in a manner which allows the beneficiary to appreciate the gift from the trust creator. Or in a way which makes the beneficiary feel guilty?

One obstacle to doing the best can be the trustee assuming the role of hero. This is all too common by attorneys who serve as trustee, but not limited to them. While attorneys are the hero in, say, accomplishing a successful result in a court trial, sometimes the better practice in various dealing with families in the trustscape is for the trustee to take more of a facilitative role, bringing the family off the sidelines and into engagement with each other or with themselves. This may be more the role of leading from

behind, which is often the approach of the *personne due confiance*. The role of hero also necessitates the roles of villain and victim. This is generally an unhealthy interdependency in families and in trusts.

A related obstacle to the trustee doing his best is considering the beneficiary as an object or, perhaps worse, as an idiot. The trustee is more often doing his best working *with* beneficiaries, not *to* them.

This is all to say that a trustee's expertise in process may be as important, and sometimes *more* important, than his substantive knowledge. Loyalty should inform all the trustee's actions, and part of that is to know where he's at and what's going on.

Chapter Twenty
Establish "What Is"

To a man with a hammer, everything looks like a nail.

~ **Mark Twain**

Why do they wait until sixth grade when you already know everything?

~ **Judy Blume, Are You There God?**
   It's Me, Margaret

And yet viewing several depictions of even an imaginary city, is enlightening in a way," Leibniz said. "Each painter can view the city from only one standpoint at a time, so he will move about the place, and paint it from a hilltop on one side, then a tower on the other, then from a grand intersection in the middle — all in the same canvas. When we look at the canvas, then, we glimpse in a small way how God understands the universe — or he sees it from every point of view at once. By populating the world with so many different minds, each with its own point of view, God gives us a suggestion of what it means to be omniscient.

~ **Attributed to Gottfried Leibniz by**
   Neal Stephenson, Quicksilver

"

An intelligence knowing all the forces acting in nature at a given instant, as well as the momentary positions of all things in the universe, would be able to comprehend in one single formula the motions of the largest bodies as well as the lightest atoms in the world, provided that its intellect were sufficiently powerful to subject all data to analysis; to it nothing would be uncertain, the future as well as the past would be present to its eyes. The perfection that the human mind has been able to give.... affords but a feeble outline of such an intelligence.

~ **Pierre-Simon Laplace**

And yet viewing several depictions of even Whoever undertakes to set himself up as a judge of Truth and Knowledge is shipwrecked by the laughter of the gods.

~ **Edmund Burke, On Empire, Liberty, and Reform: Speeches and Letters, quoting the preface to Brissot's Address to His Constituents (1794)**

"

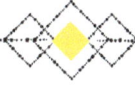

" *It sounds like a fairy-tale, but not only that; this story of what man by his science and practical inventions has achieved on this earth, where he first appeared as a weakly member of the animal kingdom, and on which each individual of his species must ever again appear as a helpless infant... is a direct fulfillment of all, or of most, of the dearest wishes in his fairy-tales. All these possessions he has acquired through culture. Long ago he formed an ideal conception of omnipotence and omniscience which he embodied in his gods. Whatever seemed unattainable to his desires — or forbidden to him — he attributed to these gods. One may say, therefore, that these gods were the ideals of his culture. Now he has himself approached very near to realizing this ideal, he has nearly become a god himself. But only, it is true, in the way that ideals are usually realized in the general experience of humanity. Not completely; in some respects not at all, in others only by halves. Man has become a god by means of artificial limbs, so to speak, quite magnificent when equipped with all his accessory organs; but they do not grow on him and they still give him trouble at times... Future ages will produce further great advances in this realm of culture, probably inconceivable now, and will increase man's likeness to a god still more.*

~ **Sigmund Freud, Civilization and Its Discontents**
"

I begin this chapter with a range of conflicting quotes simply because of the enormity of this task of defining what a trust is, and its practical impossibility. The trustee is supported in addressing this essential task by the various truths embedded in the various quotes. These truths together with the ultimate impossibility best serves as a reminder of the appropriate mindset of awe, humility, and Big Mind.

Let's begin with the simple, though not necessarily easy, and move from there.

Establish the Trust.

One of the first steps is for the trustee to know the trust document. After all, the trust document is the primary blueprint on which the trustee builds. In fact, in a real sense, *how the trustee understands the trust is how the trust will be administered.*

For trusts which are to be administered for any length of time, it can be helpful to have a written outline of the trustee's understanding of key provisions of the trust. This summary interpretation gives the trustee easier ongoing access to the terms of the trust. This summary interpretation can become the trustee's primary reference manual for the trust. As such, this serves as an efficient approach because it avoids the trustee having to repeatedly delve into the too-often hard-to-read trust document.

The writer of the interpretation may need to supplement this reference manual with additional materials beyond the trust document itself. For example, it may be necessary or helpful to

insert legal definitions and other applicable law. Families often don't understand the legal reality that their trust document lives in the laws applicable to trust. These laws are the legal framework for interpretation and fill in gaps in the trust document. Further, the law's primacy in setting public policy works to trump any contrary provisions within the trust. In Illinois, for instance, provisions which disinherit for marrying outside the faith are unenforceable.

Therefore, the trust document often cannot be fully understood without reference to the applicable trust laws. For these reasons, the trustee's interpretation of the trust should include references to the law as appropriate.

In much the same way, the trustee's interpretation of the trust should include any directives prepared by the trust creator. Directives often explain and enhance the trust creator's directions and approach as set out in his trust document. The trustee would be well advised to know what these directives provide.

It could be helpful for the trustee to establish other useful information, such as practices of the family and prior trustees as well as detail about his decisions. It may be beneficial to include other guiding documents in the process of establishing the trust, such as any Investment Policy Statement and any Distribution Policy Statement as well as any articulation of the purpose, goals, mission, and vision of the trust. This can even include the naming or renaming of the trust.[40]

---

40 Naming or renaming the trust is a practice identified by John A. Warnick in his mastery program through the Purposeful Planning Institute.

The value of the Investment Policy Statement to summarize the trust's approach to the investment of financial and other assets is well known.[41] Perhaps less well known, but of equivalent potential help is the Distribution Policy Statement (DPS). The DPS is a summary, both practical and aspirational, of the trustee's understanding of how he will view and handle distributions. The source for the DPS is the trustee's articulation of his orders from the trust creator, as well as his own decisions on how he intends to exercise any discretion he may have. This statement should coordinate with any statements of trust goals, mission, purpose, and vision of the trust.

In its creation the Distribution Policy Statement can and should generate buy-in from the beneficiary, and so can be helpful in analyzing distribution requests and in mitigating any bad feelings a denial might otherwise engender. Specifically, the trustee can use the DPS to distinguish between distribution requests which will be summarily granted. Those requests that are outside of the DPS may require revisiting both the DPS and the IPS, a cost which the requesting beneficiary may not want to assume. In my experience, a healthy structure and process around a thoughtfully-created DPS can help enhance harmony – and discourage disputes and litigation.[42]

---

41 See, for example, Sec. 6.2.2.1 The Trustee's Duties in Charles E. Rounds III, *Loring and Rounds, A Trustee's Handbook,* Aspen Publishers Online, December 1, 2014, at p. 611.

42 Consider the use of such an approach in the fact pattern described in the case of Spencer v. DiCola. Perhaps the use of a DPS might have mitigated the upset in the denial of the specific request by pointing to those requests which the trustee would alternatively grant. Another option: the trustee perhaps should have yielded to at least explore the distribution scheme requested by the beneficiary. Either or both might have led to a mediated resolution.

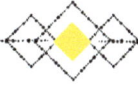

Further, it's often helpful for the trustee to share these with appropriate trust stakeholders. In fact, it may be helpful and appropriate to cocreate the policies, purposes, and goals with the beneficiaries in the right circumstance. By involving the trust stakeholders, the trustee helps create a shared understanding of "What Is." The alternative, a lack of shared understanding, is a root of conflict. If, for example, the trustee has one understanding of the trust, but the beneficiary has the opposite, there is likely to be conflict even if the trustee is legally correct. Here is an important insight into best practices: *Establishing "What Is" includes both the <u>discovery</u> of "What Is" and the <u>creation</u> of "What Is."* The task is active, and not passive. In other words, the trustee should engage in some significant *doing* in some discovery, and especially in the articulation of "What Is" is.

Where the trustee is serving first as successor trustee or is otherwise involved while the trust creator is still available, he might have a greater role in establishing the trust. First, he can confirm that the written interpretation matches the trust creator's intentions.

Second, he can confirm that the trust itself will fly, by taking part in field-testing to assess the fit and processes of the trust with the applicable stakeholders. Those who have participated in my field-testing have been enthusiastic. This could ultimately incorporate family discussions on the impact of the trust, particularly the beneficiaries' point of view.

Third, he can help in the overall organization of the trust creator to help minimize the known phenomenon of the survivor having to spend the first several months searching for things. The search includes looking for assets – such as precise identification of bank and investment accounts – as well as access to those assets, such as passwords.

Next, there's another question of what the trust does not explicitly establish. This is the vision, the psychospiritual foundation for the purpose of the trust, and the connection to the family. Often, the trustee comes into the trust without any of these policies or expressions or purpose. The masterful trustee may help the family discover and create these supporting documents.

Establish the Trust Stakeholders.

Who the players are – and aren't – is foundational. The stakeholders include the trust creator, the beneficiaries, and the trusted advisors.

Establish the Trust Creator. The trust creator may be dead or alive. If alive, he may have functional capacity or not. In addition, the trust creator's ability and willingness to be engaged is also variable. For example, some people are more able than others to seriously consider scenarios as to their own mortality or the circumstances of their beloved. These topics are often difficult and avoided in our culture. Therefore, discovery and creation are often a delicate conversation, even when the trust creator is legally competent.

If the trust does not already provide, the trustee may be well advised to assist the trust creator in the creation of purpose statements and directives. This can be particularly important in enhancing and supplementing the trust documents with the many details which can help for a smoother transition into and through the trust. Happily, more trusts are expressly designed to include the trust creator's purpose, in part to comply with the Uniform Trust Code.

Then there's a host of helpful aspects to establish, including their preferred method of learning, and their relationship to other stakeholders, and the assets of the trust and the family. Depending on resources and receptiveness, formal testing and assessments can be useful tools. There are a range of personality tests as well as those attuned to polarities and family dynamics.[43] This all establishes the trust creator as well as alignment of the vision of the trust and the vision of the family. Where the vision is less than fully developed and actuated, the trustee can be helpful in moving the family closer. Note, again, that the trustee's help in this area may look more like leadership from behind.

The idea here is that a goal or purpose is an essential to have a successful trust, or a successful trust administration. In fact, it may only be through the expression of such a goal or purpose

---

43 Personality tests include DISC, Myers-Briggs, MMPI, Strength Finders, Strong Interest Inventory, Kolbe, Hogan Development Survey, and the revived version of the ancient Enneagram. Various investment professionals offer an assessment of the individual's financial personality profile. Polarity Partnerships offered an assessment which showed where a family is in relation to any given interdependency. The Purposeful Planning Institute offered an assessment process as trustscape road map.

that there may be a consensus as to the metrics of successful trust administration.

Often this goal is far beyond mere financial goals, such as saving taxes. To be successful the trust typically provides some gift to the beneficiary, who is typically another family member. So, the purpose of the trust at its best is likely aligned with the vision of the trust creator for his family.

Establish the Beneficiaries. Who are the people and organizations standing to benefit immediately or perhaps later from the trust? What is their history and context, and their awareness and consciousness? How do they learn? What are their strengths and weaknesses? What are their dreams and goals? What is the quality and intensity of their engagement with the trust? Where are they in relation to the dreams and gravitational pull of the trust creator?

Depending on resources and receptiveness, formal testing and assessments can again be useful tools. Regardless of the assistance the trustee reasonably employs, it's often best for the trustee himself to engage firsthand with each beneficiary.

There's also the nice, if difficult question, of who may have been *excluded* as beneficiaries. They may not be expressly identified in the trust document. Can the trust creator provide insight as to why he excluded them? Do the excluded beneficiaries know they have been excluded?

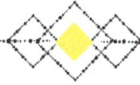

Excluded beneficiaries often bring a lawsuit motivated by their suspicion of wrongdoing, such as undue influence by an included relative, spurred by the surprise insult of their disinheritance in the context of the stress of the loss. "Mom never so much as insinuated I wouldn't receive my share." Enduring an intrafamily lawsuit can be traumatic for the individuals involved as well as the family as a whole and can deplete the trust's assets in a way that was not contemplated by the trust creator.

Where the trustee is brought in first as successor, he could do well to investigate opportunities to mitigate such exclusions. And generally, the earlier the trustee is brought in, the bigger the opportunity to engage in the best practice of connecting and collaborating with the rising generation.

Establish the Trusted Advisors. Through both their individual expertise and their relationship with the family, the trusted advisors are critical stakeholders in the success of the family and of the trust administration. Generally, the deeper and longer the relationship, the more helpful the advisor can be.

In addition to their history with the family and depth of their connection, discovery could include the boundaries and extent of their respective expertise, enlightenment, and loyalty. They may also be of help in other discovery as well as informing the trustee as to key considerations of his discretion, including his communications. Beyond discovery, the trusted advisors may be important in cocreating the ongoing collaboration through the trust. They can help establish communications and foster growth.

In the process of establishing the trusted advisors, the trustee may become aware of missing expertise. The expertise gap may exist, for example, over management as to special assets, such as insurance or real estate, or appropriately dealing with the dynamics of the family or the special considerations of any specific member.

Absent expertise may more likely include those who would service the trust creator or beneficiary directly. Would the aging trust creator benefit from bringing in a care manager sooner than later to help guide and support a smooth transition? In my practice, the trusted advisor most often not yet in place is the care manager. This professional assists with the planning, care, and administration around the present or anticipated sickness and disability of a family member, whether trust creator or beneficiary.

In the context of present or anticipated sickness and disability, other professionals include bookkeepers, bill payers, daily money managers, and those who might help with these and other activities of daily living which are getting more difficult or are simply better done by someone else. Note also that in addition to supporting the flagging skills of the trust creator, these resources also aid a smooth transition by having the replacement personnel learning directly, as opposed to later having to figure it out for themselves when the trust creator is no longer available. These financial assistants can also be helpful to develop budgeting and bill-paying skills for family members who may be assuming this role from the trust creator or otherwise becoming independent of the trust creator.

The trustee may also discover other missing competencies, less obvious to the other stakeholders. These helpful advisors can include those who facilitate family communications, family decision-making, family mediation, individual and family legacy development, and philanthropic projects. In the present culture, the value of both legacy and philanthropic projects are sorrowfully underappreciated. A developed philanthropic consciousness or legacy can powerfully help support both families and their members.

Depending on the situation, helpful experts may include those with unusual or unorthodox skills. They can also include those who will provide direct support to the trustee, such as separate legal counsel. In addition to trust advisors, the trust may involve other fiduciaries. In that event, the trustee should establish them as well.

The trustee may find a range of obstacles in bringing in any of the missing expertise. It then becomes his job to educate and develop other appropriate strategies to bring them in. The failure, for example, to bring in a care manager in advance of need may well require the hiring of a care advocate in the midst of a crisis. Generally, crisis management hinders the successful management of the trust.

Establish the Trustee. The work of the trustee in improving his own skills and awareness is ongoing as part of his loyalty to his

growth, his profession, and to his trust stakeholders. And it often seems that the trusts and stakeholders he attracts are perfectly attuned to continue that journey. Though the extent of his ability to embrace the challenges may vary, it may be helpful and wise to establish from time to time such aspects as: who am I in this trust? Who am I to each trust stakeholder?

Establish the Assets.

What are the assets of the trust? This simple direct question leads to others: What could and should be the assets of the trust? For example, what was the disposition of a project or enterprise of the family? Is there unaccounted for value in artistic or other things or intangibles?

The assets may extend beyond those which were assumed by others in compiling the trust. Stray financial assets may appear over time. More typically, the value of an asset may be inaccurately assumed – both over- and under-appreciation. This applies to businesses, land and other real estate, personal property, art, and collectables. It is usually best to obtain accurate valuations and address disposition plans while the trust creator can deal with any mistaken assumptions.

Best practices would also include the discovery of a family's non-financial assets, namely, their social, intellectual, human as well as spiritual assets. These can be helpful in establishing the trust's purpose and goals, as well as for building the vision and developing the relationship with the beneficiary.

A Further Thought on How to Establish "What Is."

The trustee may be well advised to use his own senses for the core work. In fact, there is evidence suggesting this is a responsibility which the trustee may not legally delegate to another. For example, in the remarkable Holman case[44] the judge admonished the trustee for failing to ever have a face-to-face meeting with the institutionalized and disabled minor beneficiary. The judge wisely ruled that without direct observation – which is the most basic of investigations – the trustee was not fulfilling his responsibility. As it happened, further activism by the court lead to the blossoming of the life of this institutionalized beneficiary.

The judge's conclusion in this case was not merely philosophical: the trustee's failure to investigate prevented him from acting in the best interests of the beneficiary. Only after he visited was the helpful care identified which eventually transformed this shut-in beneficiary to be active and engaged. This story highlights another essential of the trustee in performing this core task of determining what is: *the active use of the trustee's own senses as well as his common sense and intuition.*

We can see how the masterful exercise of determining "what is," supports doing what's best, and is foundational for loyalty.

---

44 This 2012 New York case involved the grantor's lawyer and a large bank who were seeking guardianship over the disabled minor beneficiary. The judge challenged whether they were operating the trust in service to the beneficiary. Rather, they were collecting their fees and growing the trust corpus, at the price of not paying for anything on behalf of the beneficiary – and hadn't visited him in years. The ruling reverberates beyond beneficiaries with disabilities and million-dollar trusts. For more information, visit the reporting on this case in a 2013 issue of *the Village Voice* at https://www.villagevoice.com/2013/07/10/the-ruling-that-could-change-everything-for-disabled-people-with-million-dollar-trusts/.

Chapter Twenty -One
Protect "What Is"

G iven the importance of loyalty, it should be no surprise that one major portion of the trustee's actions is devoted to protecting what has been entrusted to him. Protection typically includes the rear-guard action of serving as the fortress for "What Is." This is to protect from predators and other forbidden distributions.

And sometimes protection can also require calculated risk, as any prudent person may encounter. For example, the amount of resources prudent to expend in the name of protecting any given asset is a matter reasonable minds may disagree on. In addition to minimum standards that are set by law, there are best practices which the trustee may keep in mind for the benefit of the family.

Let's consider the different things and people that a trustee may typically be called upon to protect.

Protecting an Asset.

The trustee has obligations to protect both the financial as well as the non-financial assets of the family. The former obligation is recognized by law.

Protecting Financial Assets. Understand first that the protection typically has some dynamic elements to it. So, consider first someone charged with protecting another's house while they are away. The tasks for the protection would likely include care and maintenance of the physical – such as tasks ranging from mowing the lawn to replacing the roof as needed; paying for utilities,

taxes, insurance, and other necessary and prudent expenses; and providing such monitoring and guarding to reasonably look out for and prevent break-ins.

The trustee's protective function is typically not a static preservation, like housing relics in a museum, but dynamic because it is for the benefit of the ongoing needs of another. So, protecting the same house for a beneficiary, the trustee may be called upon to take on additional considerations. One example may be to make the house accessible for an increasingly less able beneficiary. Another consideration may be for a successor beneficiary, such as selling the house if the neighborhood appears to be on the decline, or in another situation, selling the property to take due advantage of rising values. Even where trust creator may not have expressly anticipated these circumstances, the trustee has to deal with them to define what is appropriate protection.

A fine example here is the case of Dr. Barnes[45] who required in the trust for his remarkable art collection to remain displayed only in his house. With the changes in the neighborhood years later along with other changed circumstances, his trustee sought court permission to move the collection. Due protection of this artistic asset resulted in the removal from the originally designated fortress to another.

---

45 For more information on this case see Debra Blum's works in the January 2005 and April 2005 issues of *The Chronicle of Philanthropy.* This case would create a new precedent for nonprofit trusts.

Barnes' case also highlights the duality of the grantor's intent and the impact on the beneficiary – his gift was not having the impact he intended. The court recognized that the public was an important beneficiary in Barnes' trust and the impact of where they were to receive the gift mattered more than Barnes' desire to keep the art in his house.

As to financial investments, the same dynamic process applies. Therefore, Policy Statements are at their best a reflection of the plan of how the money will be protected so as to be available to pay for what is needed to distribute to the beneficiaries. In so doing, Policy Statements for both Investments and Distributions support the trustee's best practice of protection.

Protecting how the money is spent is an issue on an immediate level. For example, what is our budget for the month and the year, as well as on a long-term perspective? How long will the trust assets last given projected expenses and distributions? Where there are particularly significant financial assets, the trustee aspiring to best practices may be considering more exotic protections, such as off-shore asset protection as well as daisy-chaining life insurance policies, and formal or informal family banks for supporting future family entrepreneurism, among others.

The notion of protection also is an elaboration of the idea of "do no harm." This is an important ideal to orient around, even if the impact of the trustee's actions is ultimately outside his control.

Protecting Non-Financial Assets. In addition to financial assets, the trustee on the mastery journey should protect the non-financial assets, including intellectual, human, social, and spiritual.[46] This is true even though these non-financial assets may not be expressly contained in the inventory of the trust, and the trustee's legal responsibilities may formally end with the protection of financial assets.

Applying Polarity Thinking, the wealth of a family can be revealed as a multarity, where each of these asset categories, financial and otherwise, is essential, and none are sufficient on their own. In fact, some don't even consider financial assets to be the most important, or rather, that financial assets are only in service for the other assets. This relative placement of finances is evidenced by the advisor's insightful question to the trust creator: if you had to give up one asset, which would it be? Often the trust creator, in this exercise, agrees to surrender his wealth, because with the other assets, he can regain the financial.

Jay Hughes demonstrates this principle by using his hand, each finger representing an asset, the thumb equating with financial assets. With the hand positioned so the thumb is facing down, supporting the other fingers, Jay demonstrates a healthy balance. He demonstrates an unhealthy balance by having the thumb take the lead from the other fingers.

---

46 These non-financial assets are generally recognized. Jay Hughes and Richard Orlando, among others, have provided greater clarity around these.

The trustee's recognition of financial assets as supportive of the other assets of the trust creator and beneficiaries informs how and why he protects the financial assets. The masterful trustee recognizes the protection of financial assets is not a be-all and end-all purpose, but rather lives in service to the other assets. This principle may be manifested in the statements of the Mission and Goals of the Trust, as well as in the Policy Statements for Investments and, especially, Distributions.

In this way, the trustee also complies with his legal responsibilities for protecting the financial assets AND with his, at least, equally important moral role of protecting the values, skills, and legacy of the family.

Protecting People.

As challenging as it can be to protect an inert asset, there are even more issues in protecting people.

Protecting the Trust Creator. Consider first protecting the trust creator. Let's review issues for the trust creator in reverse chronological order to better understand some of the key issues.

After the death of the trust creator, the loyal trustee protects what remains. To the extent not already completed, he should establish the trust, the beneficiaries, stakeholders, and assets, as discussed above, as well as the communication structures, as discussed following. If involved before the trust creator's death,

the trustee may be able to help with other preparations to smooth this ultimate transition.

In addition to the charge to make sure the trust creator's wishes are carried out through the trust, the trustee may have responsibilities as to the trust creator's burial and transition out of this life.

Continuing in reverse chronological order, consider the incapacity of the trust creator. With the onset of incapacity,[47] the trustee may be able to protect the trust creator by making sure his assets are being used as he wanted. This can also involve protecting the trust creator from predators and those who would take advantage of his feebleness for their own ends. The trustee may also have a role in working with those responsible for health care – the guardian, the holder of the health care, power of attorney, or the care manager.

Generally, the trustee may protect by helping to coordinate the budget with the health care fiduciary, as well as more narrowly help with the available funds and benefits. His role of protection can start with coordination of funds and benefits and expand into protection of health. Through establishing "what is," he may determine that something additional may be of help to the incapacitated trust creator. Depending on the documents and law, he may be able to purchase that helpful service or item, even if the health care fiduciaries don't request it.

---

47 Determining the onset of incapacity may not be an easy thing. In some jurisdictions, it may be voluntarily assumed. In others, it may be subject to a medical or court determination, or both. In court, the determination of capacity is too often a costly and time-consuming adversarial battle, sometimes dividing the family.

Typically, there is a lack of express governance with that person. In other words, there is usually no formal structure bringing together the trustee and this other for united decision-making. Instead, there is the potential for them to each go in different directions. Too often the family emotions at time of the trust creator's incapacity are raw from both the understandably trying healthcare situation, but also because of the surprise of the first disclosure of the delegation of responsibilities, backup processes, and fiduciary structures. The trustee can serve to calm and reassure, in no small part by ongoing, impartial, and sensitive communications. In so doing, the trustee not only protects the incapacitated trust creator, but also family harmony and family collaboration.

Where the trustee is involved in anticipation of the trust creator's incapacity, his efforts to protect may encompass consideration of the transition, particularly including how the incapacity is to be determined. The default determination of incapacity through an adversary court proceeding can be horrific, pitting family members against each other as to those who feel they are loyal to the trust creator in defending his sanity, and those who feel they are loyal by preventing the trust creator from being a danger to himself.

Alternative procedures are not perfect either. As one example, a doctor's determination may err on the side of competency, especially given the known phenomenon of the patient acting

healthily in examination. And the current culture does not yet deeply support our voluntarily turning over the car keys and other accoutrements of our freedom.

Before the incapacity of the trust creator, the trustee may be able to protect the trust creator in as many ways as the trust creator may allow. This may include serving as *personne de confiance* and generally serving as a trusted advisor with sufficient integrity to tell the truth to power.

Especially as successor trustee, the trustee can help protect the trust creator in his preparation for transition, in establishing the trust and his statement of wishes, and in otherwise planning for the transfer of control. The successor trustee protects the trust creator, his assets, and the objects of his affection by inviting the trust creator as appropriate to communicate deeply with his beneficiaries.

In sum, there can be a lot the trustee can do to protect the trust creator, including in advance of disability and death.

Protecting the Beneficiaries. The trustee protects the beneficiaries by helping with the smooth transition of the trust creator. After all, this is an understandably difficult time even if the beneficiaries are prepared intellectually and emotionally – and too many aren't. It's also understandable, and not necessarily a fault for them to be thinking about security for the trust assets.

Sometimes the trust puts the trustee squarely in the position of protecting the beneficiary from himself. These situations include so-called spendthrift trusts and incentive trusts. Administering such a trust can be a delicate and difficult project, especially if the beneficiary does not agree that he needs protecting, or worse, where the beneficiary becomes entrenched in the destructive drama where he plays the victim to the trustee's role of villain.[48] Helping the beneficiary caught in these snares to embark on his own hero's journey out of victimhood is no easy task.[49] Yet, that ultimately may be the most valuable protection that the trustee could provide: protection against a life burdened by a cloak of victimhood. The trustee is well advised to take due advantage of every support and resource available.

Even outside of trusts established to protect the beneficiary from himself, often there is at least an unstated role of the trustee to protect the beneficiary from the trust creator. This is not just through attempts to mitigate a punitive or not well-thought-out trust. Paradoxically, the protection can be needed because of the fact of the trust itself, that the ancestor is still directing the beneficiary after death, or merely because of the gravitational pull of the trust creator, which may not find direct expression in the trust document. Specifically, that the success of the vision and life of the ancestor can stand in the way of the beneficiary

---

48 This multarity is completed by the addition of the hero. In the all-too-common vicious cycle that follows, the hero role may be played by the now absent ancestor, and so remains missing.

49 Jay Hughes, for one, thinks that there is no rescuing many who come under the extraordinary force of an ancestor's gravitational field.

establishing his own vision and life.[50] At its worst, the beneficiary is unable to individuate.

The crippling of the beneficiary is often blamed on himself, for a failure of either will or the intention to take responsibility for his own life. While it's essential for the beneficiary, like anyone else, to exercise sufficient will and responsibility, these voices of blame often underestimate the consuming and powerful force of the ancestor, sometimes even rising to the level of a perfect storm. Polarity Thinking helps reveal the depth of this paradox. In order to take due care of the trust creator and his vision, Polarity Thinking compels the trustee to also protect and take care of the beneficiary. Taking due care of the beneficiary is the single largest opportunity for improving current practices in trust administration. After all, the term "beneficiary" demands that the trust provide a "benefit," which must by definition look to the subjective world of the beneficiary.

Recall also that the science of Polarity Thinking proves that the only way to achieve the trust creator's vision is to also consider how the trust will improve the life of the beneficiaries. In other words, a masterful trustee is *required* to engage in blessing the beneficiaries and is *forbidden* to blindly apply the words of the trust against the beneficiary. Of course, these aspirations to serve the beneficiary rise above the legal minimum requirements and

---

50 This is the contention of the authors in their excellent treatise on the Voice of the Rising Generation. And of Jamie Weiner in his theory of "standing in the shadow of giants."

may invite him to take steps to soften, and sometimes even to modify, the trust's language to the extent permissible under the law and reasonable under the circumstances.

More simply, the trustee protects the beneficiary by acknowledging the impact of the trust on the beneficiary's journey. When the trustee loyally pursues an administration mindful of this impact, the trustee best serves all stakeholders and the intentions of the trust.

Chapter Twenty-Two
Protect "What Is"

> *The **good** attorney returns the client's phone call the same day;*
>
> *The **very good** attorney returns the client's call within a couple of hours;*
>
> *The **great** attorney calls first.*
>
> *~ **Advice to a young lawyer***

The reason to communicate is to be a great trustee for the stakeholders. That's because excellent communication skills are inseparable components from the practices in the master trustee's playbook. Every practice in the Trustee's Playbook has a communication element. For one, the trustee's actions may not be recognized as doing what's best, let alone accomplishing what's best, without confirming through communications. The same applies to his actions of protecting and establishing "what is." Finally, it is difficult to imagine how a trustee might ever build trust and foster growth without communication. Therefore, communication is essential for the masterful trustee.

Also evidencing the fundamental importance of communication is the therapist's truism that what is not expressed often is acted out. Recalling the huge emotional component of family communications around money suggests the prudence of allowing space for full expression.

Having established the "Why" of the trustee's need to communicate, we can now address the technical aspects. Perhaps the most basic concern is HOW to communicate. Much has been written on the subject, and it's hoped there is a general appreciation, if not active development of this practice. The elements include listening skills – such as active listening, emotional intelligence, appreciative inquiry, and big mind, among others.

Less acknowledged, but just as essential is the TIMING and FREQUENCY for sharing information. Most professionals err on the sparse side. In fact, complaints about communication – particularly not returning phone calls – consistently rank among the highest complaints against attorneys by their clients. A trustee's need for communication can be considered more demanding than those of an attorney, if just because of the number of beneficiaries and key stakeholders whose involvement in any particular trust matter may warrant the sharing of information.

Excellent timing and frequency of communications can stave off many problems by helping the recipients to understand exactly what is going on, as opposed to what they expect – or fear – is going on. The dramatic Judeo-Christian example is the

construction of the golden calf, which was in part inspired by the lack of communication from Moses, who had been gone for some 40 days. The counterargument that this incident demonstrated the lack of faith of the children of Israel could benefit from recalling the sound advice attributed to President Ronald Reagan: "Trust, but verify." Verification is through timely communication.

Timing may sometimes suggest the communication comes before the trustee's action. The trustee's advising in advance of a decision may be prudent. Consider, for example, the trustee advising the applicable stakeholders that he will be selling the family house in such and such a manner. This advance communication keeps the stakeholders advised, sets their expectations as to timing and process and results, and allows for the addressing of any objections, should they arise. The benefit extends defensively here as well. Those who may later complain should be silenced by the simple counter: you should have said something when I let you know before I acted.

Trustees are known to adopt the minimum communication frequency required by law. Though that may lead to their vindication in a lawsuit, the fact of the lawsuit may have been a failure of employing best practices as to the timing and frequency of communications. For instance, the law may require but a single accounting per year. However, some trustees may appropriately provide ongoing access to bank account reconciliations, or through technology, may provide ongoing view-only access to

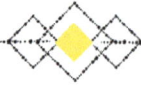

accounts through the Internet. I've found that beneficiaries are understandably reassured by such ongoing access.

The practice of setting a cadence or rhythm in communications is a subtler aspect of timing and frequency. This practice is especially beneficial during a project. As an example, setting a weekly update at a fixed date and time during a decanting process may keep the stakeholders well informed and on-track. Cadence applies in the ordinary scheme of things, even if it's merely around an annual meeting. A dependable cadence builds trust.

The trustee on the road to mastery should also consider the subjective perspective of the person with whom he's in dialogue. This perspective entails a cluster of elements. With the family members, both trust creators and beneficiaries, communication elements could include the expectations of the other – how and what are they looking to dialogue about as well as their preferred modality, such as, texting, phone, in-person, and email – and the ability of the other to hear – their education, sophistication, learning style, personality and their current availability to consider a trust issue.

Therefore, the masterful trustee would do well to consider the differences between people, and who is receiving the communication. The overly objective context of the trustee often ignores the dramatically subjective viewpoint of both the trust creator and the beneficiary: this is their family and their life, after all. Stories abound of the trustee who drops dramatic information

regarding a trust's impactful provision on a beneficiary in a routine manner of a waiter listing the day's offering. Successful approaches may instead include explicit discussions on communication preferences and learning styles, as well as considerate approaches, such as those offered through a system like Appreciative Inquiry.

The differences between the speaker and the listener are to be appreciated for other reasons. Two different people are said to make up two separate worlds. Even if speaking the same language, the differences in people between subjective and cultural filters can be enormous. As a meta consideration, the trustee may be wise to consider BOTH the particular Spiral Dynamic's meme of the listener and the meme in which the message lives. All these attributes of the participants to the communication must be established through the practice of Determining "What Is." The trustee should know himself, as well as the other participant(s). That knowledge is necessarily incremental and often best described as a dance.

It's said that context is everything. In addition to the subjective aspects of the listener, the trustee should appreciate the context of the communication. That context particularly includes the energetic language as well as the framing. For one example, the trustee might consider whether a given issue might be better framed as an Opportunity as opposed to a Problem.[51]

---

51 Ian McDermott well set out my first exposure to the framing distinction of Problem vs. Opportunity in his talk at the 2013 Rendezvous of the Purposeful Planning Institute.

Consideration of these elements may affect the form and manner of communications as well as their timing. Among other elements, the trustee on the road to mastery should consider the wisdom offered through the paradigm of the Five Energies. This paradigm suggests the value of constructing communications which leverage other modalities besides the intellectual. In addition to the already mentioned sensitivity to the emotional valence of the communication, the trustee might reinforce the communication by connecting to

- *The spiritual*, which may be around vision or religious;

- *The psychological*, which may be around the relation of the listener to one or more people or things; and/or

- *The physical*, which may implicate the setting in which the communication is made and the elements beyond words.

As to the last, one option is the use of physically walking through the applicable Polarity Map.® The use of apparel and accessories of family members at an annual meeting to indicate membership in the various dimensions of a family works on both the psychological as well as physical dimensions of communication.[52]

The importance of communications strongly suggests that communication breakdowns be duly addressed. There are many remediation approaches, such as those which attempt to retrace

---

52 Hughes describes this practice in his book *Family Wealth*.

the faulty communication by distinguishing between the speaker's good intention and his speech's negative impact. And, of course, the SUBJECT MATTER of the communications is important. Besides dealing with the tasks at hand, the trustee can reinforce alignment and purpose. Further, communication on any subject may also build rapport and relationship, thus strengthening trustworthiness, including appropriate doses of what otherwise might be considered off topic, such as personal sharing and small talk. The trustee should not let his thoughtful plans diminish his authentic and personable communication.

Communication systems and approach may be properly an element of a trustee's engagement agreement. Revisiting the impact and manner of communications can also be a constructive agenda item for the annual meeting.

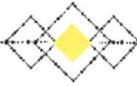

Chapter Twenty-Three
Build Trust

In contrast to communicating, building trust and enhancing trustworthiness are skills that are rarely taught, and even less often practiced. Typically, this is discussed as avoiding violations of trust, such as not committing conflicts of interest and being free from distractions. While avoiding conflicts and distractions is essential, the practice of building trust is much more than that.

Simply put, conflicts of interest evidence the absence of loyalty. A trustee's conflict of interest communicates powerfully and destructively. The destructive power of a conflict of interest is so great that even the *appearance* of a conflict should be avoided. This is why trustees are often forbidden to have business dealings with the trust – such as buying the trust family's house – even where they can demonstrate that they are paying market price or above.

At one level, conflicts exist legally and objectively, such as the example above. All too often these can have devastating consequences for both the trust and the family. The horror stories aren't just about an evil trustee. In fact, court records prove that the beloved trusted advisor can fall into this trap.[53] At another level, the trustee concerned about best practices may also be sensitive to the subjective feelings of the key stakeholders about conflicts. For example, a family may feel more comfortable if the trustee is not also employed as the investment manager for the trust. As

---

53 See, for example, the litigation involving the noted Chicago attorney and fiduciary, Marshall Eisenberg 669 F.3d 838 (7th Cir. 2012). A summary and analysis can be found at http://goo.gl/FD725K

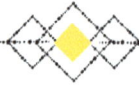

another, the family may prefer the trustee not to charge on an assets-under-management basis, where they want to make sure the trustee distributes funds in amounts appropriate to support the family's other assets.

Distractions may not rise to the level of a conflict of interest, but may signal a lack of presence, and therefore tend to undermine the experience of loyalty. For instance, a trustee who tends to other tasks over trust tasks may undermine loyalty.

Beyond conflicts and distractions, the Trustee's Playbook includes known practices such as integrity – doing what you say, and saying what you do. Note the essential ingredient of communication once again.

The best practice includes the express articulation of trust building as a goal of the trustee, including acknowledging situations which confirm trust, and perhaps more important, anticipating and dealing directly with those inevitable situations which tend to undermine trust. This should start through express mention in the retainer agreement and continue as a theme throughout the administration. Merely apologizing may be an inadequate repair. Rather, it should be seen as an opportunity to make good and to learn, which can be helpful in communication and managing the trust.

Chapter Twenty-Four
Foster Growth

My approach through this book has been to treat enlightened trust administration as a journey. It's a journey for the trustee as well as for the family. In fact, part of a trustee's journey is accompanying a family on their life's journey. He may also travel along for stretches with various trusted advisors.

A key part of a successful life's journey is growth. This can be a growth in maturity and in wisdom, as well as just age. It's growth through learning through positive experiences as well as painful ones. Growth is an interdependent pair with Establishing "What Is." Thus, the enlightened trustee is conscious of his own growth as well as the growth of those he's working with. In fact, these paths may be intertwined.

As demonstrated so far, the trustee may be well advised to grow and develop in skills having to do with trust building, communications, personality assessments, and project management. These also include the other tools, skills and mindsets of the trustee set out in Section Two. Learning these practices goes along with the other technical learning as to trusts, taxes, project management, budgets, and budgeting.

To a real extent, the trustee's engagement in this learning will inevitably spill over to those whom he works with. He may be able to involve them more directly in this growth as well. This is true especially where the empowerment and enlightenment of the beneficiaries is expressly part of the trustee's job. And it

also can happen where it's not. In fact, the trustee may establish growth as a goal in the process of Establishing the Trust.

This practice may bring the trustee's role into being a mentor,[54] educator, and facilitator, as well as fellow student.

---

54 For more about trustee mentorship, consider the article by Jay Hughes, "Trustee as Mentor" at www.jamesehughes.com/articles/trusteementor.pdf

Chapter Twenty-Five
Further Thoughts on Approaching the Playbook

The Nature of a Practice.

Engaging in a practice is different from other work. Consistent with the discussion on Growth, above, a practice involves ongoing and incremental learning. The net effect is often greater than the sum of its parts, due to the benefits of internalizing increasing sections of the process.

I've experienced the learning not as a simple straight line, but rather as a flowering, especially through various challenges. In addition to talking to a trust's stakeholders on these issues, I've found other colleagues and resources helpful.[55] I've found the ongoing study from monthly roundtables particularly beneficial along with larger annual gatherings.

Often Non-delegable.

The trustee benefits from personal engagement in the various aspects of this work, including serving as at least one of the front-line participants as much as reasonably possible. This is the interdependent pair of Depth AND Breadth. This approach tends to maximize the results and growth. This approach also best prepares a trustee for the exercise of judgment and discretion,

---

55 Even just within the trustscape, these are too numerous to mention.

which the law often does not permit a trustee to delegate to others, nor should it.

Simultaneity.

These practices overlap and often have to be dealt with at once.

Some of this is helpful and inevitable. For example, good communication can simultaneously help establish what is, enhance a stakeholder's feeling of being protected, and enhance trust and growth. The trustee should be in search of methods which achieve multiple results simultaneously.

The Limits of "What Is," Especially Time and Money.

There's a practical boundary that trustee's necessarily encounter. This boundary pushes against the "best result," though it can helpfully mitigate against the paralysis of analysis. Ultimately, the trustee is aided here by the law which typically looks most closely at the *process* of the trustee's decision. Keep a good record of the elements addressed.

Of note, I do NOT contend that the list of practices articulated in this book must be part of that record.

Simple, But Not Easy.

Need I say more?

Afterword

My work as a Trustee is grounded in the particulars of circumstances, including being spiritually informed by aspects of the Jewish faith and various wisdoms, especially that from Abraham Joshua Heschel.

I referenced Heschel's foundational contribution to the study of polarities. Among other key facets, his observations weren't limited to the intellectual. He devoted himself to maintaining the strength and equilibrium of opposing poles in order to maintain a wholesome whole, which is one of the reasons he walked on the front lines with the Reverand Martin Luther King, Jr.

Heschel keenly noted in his writing "No Time for Neutrality" the challenges inherent in the polarized aspects of prayer:

> *These principles are the two poles about which Jewish prayer revolves. Since each of the two moves in the opposite direction, equilibrium can only be maintained if both are of equal force. However, the pole of regularity usually proves to be stronger than the pole of spontaneity, and, as a result, there is a perpetual danger of prayer becoming a mere habit, a mechanical performance, an exercise in repetitiousness. The fixed pattern and regularity of our services tends to stifle the spontaneity of devotion [and intention]. Our great problem, therefore, is how not to let the principle of regularity impair the power of devotion [kavanah]. It is a problem that concerns not only prayer but also the whole sphere of ... observance."*

Heschel's warning about prayer applies to trust administration. It's the same challenge Hartley Goldstone addressed in his cautionary tale of the trustee who mistook his checklist for wisdom. Responding to this challenge has been the essential truth of my practice for more than three decades. I am grateful that I offer my whole being as trustee to families in all aspects of their trust.

I have been grounded in this through my learnings. This in no way means I push my beliefs upon those I serve. Rather, it allows me to travel the journey with them and beside them, learning or teaching as the need arises. And it sheds light ahead when the path is not clear.

I take to heart that this work is more than just lip service and pushing papers. And I believe that every trustee in the search of mastery needs to find their ground to rest their feet. I have offered up my take and interpretation of and practice within the trustscape. It has served me and those I serve well. I hope you take from this book what you can and serve your clients with excellence and compassion, as I have always sought to do.

Thank you for opening your mind to new theories of practice.

Bibliography

ACTEC. 2005. "What it Means to be a Trustee: A Guide for Clients." *ACTEC Journal*, 31(1), Summer 2005. American College of Trust and Estate Counsel (ACTEC), Fiduciary Matters Subcommittee.

Bank of Manhattan Company. 1925. *The Biography of an Idea… Trusteeship, Ancient and Modern*, 2nd Edition. New York: Bank of Manhattan Company, Trust Department.

Beaulier, Patrick. 2013, January 21. "Kavanah vs. Keva In Jewish Prayer." Punk Torah. https://punktorah.org/kavanah-vs-keva-in-jewish-prayer/

Blum, Debra E. 2005, January 6. "Court Ruling Could Influence Restrictions Donors Place on Bequests." *The Chronicle of Philanthropy*.

Blum, Debra E. 2005, April 28. "Pennsylvania's Highest Court Allows Multibillion-Dollar Art Collection to Move." *The Chronicle of Philanthropy*.

Brown, Kathy. 2006. *A Different Perspective: A Passionate Journey*. Bloomington: AuthorHouse.

Brown, Kathy. 2008. *The Secret to the Zone*, Book 1. Bloomington: AuthorHouse.

Brown, Kathy. 2008. *The Secret to the Zone: Intellectual Energy*, Book 2. Bloomington: AuthorHouse.

Buber, Martin. 1937 (2010, reprint). *I-Thou*. Martino Fine Books.

Chast, Ron. 2014. *Can't We Talk about Something More Pleasant*. London: Bloomsbury.

Cialdini, Professor Robert. 2009. *Influence: Science and Practice*, 5th Edition. London: Pearson.

Collins, Jim. 2001. *Good to Great*. Harper Business.

Comins, Mike. 2024. https://www.rabbimikecomins.com

Cooperrider, David and Diana Whitney. 2005. *Appreciative Inquiry: A Positive Revolution in Change*. Oakland: Berrett-Koehler Publishers.

Davidson, Richard J. and Antoine Lutz. 2008, January 1. "Buddha's Brain: Neuroplasticity and Meditation." *IEEE Signal Process Magazine*, 25(1): 176–174.

Duncan, John and Anita M. Sarafa. 2011. "Achieve the Promise-and Limit the Risk-of Multi-Participant Trusts." *ACTEC Law Journal*, 36 (4), Spring 2011.

Felix, Daniel P. 2014, 2024. "Field-Testing A Trust for Success" https://the-professional-trustee.com/field-testing-a-trust-for-success/

Felix, Daniel P. 2017, 2023. "Black Sheep Come in Many Colors." https://the-professional-trustee.com/black-sheep-come-in-many-colors/

Gallo, Jon J., Eileen Gallo, and James Grubman. 2010. "The Use and Abuse of Incentive Trusts: Improvements and Alternatives." The Alchemia Group. https://www.thealchemiagroup.com/wp-content/uploads/2014/06/Gallo-Gallo-and-Grubman-Article-for-Heckerling-v11-17-20101.pdf

Goldstone, Hartley. 2011, September 10. "On becoming an Excellent Trust Beneficiary." *ISSUU*. https://issuu.com/pinkcollar/docs/on-becoming-an-excellent-trust-beneficiary-2011

Goldstone, Hartley. 2012, February 12. "The Trustee who mistook his checklist for wisdom." Wealth Management. https://www.wealthmanagement.com/estate-planning/trustee-who-mistook-his-checklist-wisdom

Goldstone, Hartley. 2012. *Trustworthy: New Angles on Trusts from Beneficiaries and Trustees: A Positive Story Project showcasing beneficiaries and trustees.* CreateSpace Independent Publishing Platform.

Goldstone, Hartley, James E. Hughes Jr., and Keith Whitaker. 2015. *Family Trusts: A Guide for Beneficiaries, Trustees, Trust Protectors, and Trust Creators.* Hoboken: Bloomberg Wiley.

Goldstone, Hartley, Scotty McLennan, and Keith Whitaker. 2013, May 14. "The Moral Core of Trusteeship: How to develop fiduciary character." Wealth Management. https://www.wealthmanagement.com/client-relations/moral-core-trusteeship

Graves, Clare W. 1974. "Human Nature Prepares for a Momentous Leap." *The Futurist*, 72-87.

Greenleaf Center. 2024. "What is Servant Leadership?" Greenleaf Center for Servant Leadership. https://greenleaf.org/what-is-servant-leadership/

Hanh, Thich Nhat. 2010. *You Are Here: Discovering the Magic of the Present Moment.* Shambhala Publications.

Heschel, Abraham Joshua. 1954 (1998, reprint). *Man's Quest for God: Studies in Prayer and Symbolism*. Santa Fe: Aurora Press.

Heschel, Abraham Joshua. 1997. *Moral Grandeur and Spiritual Audacity: Essays*. New York: Farrar, Straus, and Giroux.

Holman case. 2012. Slip opinion at https://law.justia.com/cases/new-york/other-courts/2012/2012-ny-slip-op-22387.html

Hughes, Jr., James E. 1998. "Trustee as Mentor." The James E. Hughes, Jr. Foundation. https://jehjf.org/the-trustee-as-mentor/

Hughes, Jr., James E. 2002. "A Reflection on the Art and Practice of Ritual within a Family Governance System." The James E. Hughes, Jr. Foundation. https://static1.squarespace.com/static/562bfb3ce4b022641da90dbb/t/56c0b71a7da24f34f613b2da/1455470362640/Ritual.pdf

Hughes, Jr., James E. 2004. *Family Wealth, Keeping it in the Family: How Family Members and Their Advisors Preserve Human, Intellectual and Financial Assets for Generations*. New York: Bloomberg Press.

Hughes, Jr., James E. 2007. *Family: The Compact Among Generations*. New York: Bloomberg Press.

Hughes, Jr., James E. 2023. "A Reflection on the Nature and Practice of the Role of the *Personne de Confiance* in a System of Family Governance; Historically and Today." The James E. Hughes, Jr. Foundation. https://jehjf.org/a-reflection-on-the-nature-and-practice-of-the-role-of-the-personne-de-confiance-in-a-system-of-family-governance-historically-and-today/

Hughes, Jr., James E. and Patricia M. Angus. 1999. "The Trustee as Regent Within a Family Governance System." Angus Advisory Group. https://angusadvisorygroup.com/wp-content/uploads/2015/12/Regent.pdf

Hughes, Jr., James E., Susan Massenzio, and Keith Whitaker. 2014. *The Voice of the Rising Generation: Family Wealth and Wisdom*. New York: Bloomberg Press.

Illinois Statutory custodial claim. 755 ILCS 5/18-1.1 https://www.ilga.gov/legislation/ilcs/ilcs4.asp? DocName=075500050HArt%2E+XVIII&ActID=2104&ChapterID=60&SeqStart=21600000&SeqEnd=233 00000

Illinois. Illinois Rules of Professional Responsibility. https://www.illinoiscourts.gov/rules/supreme-court-rules?a=viii

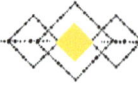

Irvine, William B. 2009. *A Guide to the Good Life: The Ancient Art of Stoic Joy*. Oxford: Oxford University Press.

Johnson, Barry. 1975. *Polarity Management: Identifying and Managing Unsolvable Problems*. Pelham: HRD Press.

Johnson, Barry. 2020. *And: Making a difference by Leveraging Polarity, Paradox or Dilemma*. Pelham: HRD Press.

Langbridge Case. 1975. Common Bench 1345, reported Yearbook, 19 Edw. III 375 according to George Anastaplo, *Human Being and Citizen, Essays on Virtue, Freedom and the Common Good*. Swallow Press.

Lyubomirsky, Sonja. 2008. *The How of Happiness: A New Approach to Getting the Life You Want*. London: Penguin Books.

Maimonides, Moses. 1135-1204 (1956, reprinted). *The Guide for the Perplexed*. London: Routledge & K. Paul.

Major League Baseball. 2024. "The Official Rules of Major League Baseball." https://www.mlb.com/

Merkle, John C. 2009. *Approaching God: The Way of Abraham Joshua Heschel*. Liturgical Press.

O'Sullivan, Timothy P. 2007. "Family Harmony: An all too frequent casualty of the estate planning process." *Marquette Elder's Advisor*, 8(2), Spring 2007, 257-258.

Orlando, Richard J. 2013. *Legacy: The Hidden Keys to Optimizing Your Family Wealth Decisions*. Legacy Capitals Press.

Payne, Alexander, Director. 2011. *The Descendants*. Fox Searchlight Productions.

Plaut, W. Gunther, editor. 1981. *Torah: A Modern Commentary*. Union of American Hebrew Congregations.

Polarity Partnerships. 2024. Polarity Mastery Programs and Certification. Ongoing training. Polarity Partnerships. https://www.polaritypartnerships.com/

Purposeful Planning Institute. 2024. Annual Rendezvous and Mastery Program. Ongoing trainings. Purposeful Planning Institute. https://purposefulplanninginstitute.com/

Raphael, Simcha Paull. 2013. "Images of Joseph's Bones in Torah and Midrash." Da'at Institute. http://www.daatinstitute.net/wp-content/uploads/2013/04/JosephsBonesDAAT.pdf

Raphael, Simcha Paull. 2015. *Living and Dying in Ancient Times: Death, Burial, and Mourning in Biblical Tradition.* Boulder: Albion-Andalus Books.

Reiner, Rob, Director. 1992. *A Few Good Men.* Columbia Pictures.

Riley, James G. 2014, October 31. Panel discussion by James G. Riley, Supervising Judge, Circuit Court of Cook County, Probate Division. Hosted by Advocate Charitable Foundation and Northern Trust.

Rounds III, Charles E. 2014. *Loring and Rounds, A Trustee's Handbook.* Aspen Publishers Online.

Royce, Josiah. 1908 (1995, reprint). *The Philosophy of Loyalty,* Edited by John J. McDermott. Nashville: Vanderbilt University Press.

Savchuk, Katia. 2013, July 10. "The Ruling That Could Change Everything for Disabled People with Million-Dollar Trusts." *The Village Voice.* https://www.villagevoice.com/2013/07/10/the-ruling-that-could-change-everything-for-disabled-people-with-million-dollar-trusts/

Scanlon v. Eisenberg. 2012. 669 F.3d 838 (7th Cir. 2012). A summary and analysis can be found at http://www.jcblawyer.com/for-estate-trust-guardianship-litigation/too-many-hats-the-dangers-of-a-trustee-acting-in-multiple-additional-roles-from-a-recent-and-very-real-lawsuit-and-the-continuing-dramatic-saga/

Schuman, Amy, John L. Ward, and Stacy Stutz. 2010. *Family Business as Paradox.* Palgrave: MacMillan Press.

Schwartz, Barry and Ken Sharpe. 2011. *Practical Wisdom: The Right Way to Do the Right Thing.* New York: Riverhead Books.

Shapiro, Rabbi Rami. 2010. *Tanya, the Masterpiece of Hasidic Wisdom: selections annotated and explained.* SkyLight Illuminations.

Sinek, Simon. 2009, September. "How great leaders inspire action." TEDxPuget Sound. https://www.ted.com/talks/simon_sinek_how_great_leaders_inspire_action

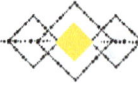

Spencer v. DiCola. 2014. Ill. App. (1st) 121173, 2014 Ill app LEXIS 289 (1st Dist. 5/1/14), rehearing denied, August 18, 2014, modified on denial of rehearing, 2014 Ill. App. (1st) 121585, 16 N.E.3d 1 (August 21, 2014).

Thurber, Marshall. 2014, October 23. "Predicting the Unexpected." TEDxMelbourne. https://youtu.be/m1Lka28V-vo

Welles, Orson, Director. 1941. *Citizen Kane*. Mercury Productions.

Wesley, Matt. 2014, December 1. "Culture Does Indeed Eat Structure for Lunch." The Wesley Group. https://www.thewesleygroup.com/blog/?p=609

White, Peter. 2006. *Ecology of Being*. All In All Books.

Wilber, Ken. 2000. *Integral Psychology: consciousness, Spirit, Psychology, Therapy*. Shambhala Publications.

Wolf, Arnold Jacob. 1998. "Keva and Kavanah: How the balance of keva (routine) and kavanah (intention) inform Judaism and the thought of Abraham Joshua Heschel." My Jewish Learning. https://www.myjewishlearning.com/article/keva-kavvanah/

Acknowledgments

To all the wonderful clients who I have served, I am grateful for the lessons and the opportunity to aid in managing their family legacy – financial and otherwise.

I continue to be blessed with a tremendously talented and dedicated team, especially my colleague of 20+ years, *Teresa Kritsas*, who has copiloted so much of the trustee journey.

There are many colleagues whose work has shed great light on the path for me and others, as mentors and practitioners passionately engaged in the journey. The short and noninclusive list includes:

Peter White and *Jay Hughes*, *giants whose shoulders I stand on.*

Hartley Goldstone, *who published one of my trust success stories and who facilitated the development of the trustee telos during one of his workshops at the Purposeful Planning Institute's Rendezvous.*

John A. Warnick *and his Purposeful Planning Community.*

Kathy Brown *and her work with the Five Energies and ongoing consultations.*

Gary Shunk, *who considers financial decisions to consist primarily around the emotional.*

Kevin Quinn *and the Independent Trustee Alliance.*

Thanks to *Mitchell Kupferberg, JD, LSW*, *for helping with the distinction of loyalty to Self vs. self.*

I gratefully acknowledge the generous and gracious support and help of *Barry Johnson*, creator of Polarity Thinking® theory, practice, and tools, and cofounder and principal of Polarity Partnerships, LLC., and his colleagues, cofounder *Leslie DePol*, and *Susan Dupre* and *W. Cliff Kayser*. See www.Polarity Partnerships.com. I also gratefully acknowledge the editing help of Polarity Thinking collaborator, *Neesa Sweet* from Braided River Group. See www.braidedrivergroup.com.

To my book editor, *Bonniejean Alford* of Alford Enterprises, and my designer, *Debra Kocis* of Envision Impact, Inc., I remain eternally thankful for the beauty you helped birth in the transformation of my book dream into reality.

Finally, last but certainly not least, I recognize my family for giving me specific context, meaning, and humility. Watching my parents deal with their parents' legacy as well as their own, and my children who perhaps remain to be convinced.

About the Author

*D*aniel P. Felix has been serving families as a Trustee for more than thirty years as the principal of his well-staffed law firm. Rated as a "Super Lawyer" for many years, Dan and his team have successfully managed a wide variety of trusts and have become a go-to resource for supporting smooth transitions, including for difficult and unusual trust situations.

Certified as a Master Trustee since 2019 by the Independent Trustee Alliance, Dan's primary work involves serving as a successor trustee as well as power of attorney and executor for those who want to do what they can in advance to enjoy an easier transition for themselves and their loved ones. His unique Preparedness Program enables Dan and his team to hit-the-ground running at a family's time of need. Dan also steps in as a replacement trustee, often for families who have fallen into crisis over the administration of their trusts. He prides himself as serving as an experienced, impartial, resourceful, and efficient trustee geared toward crisis resolution and returning trust management to the right track.

Daniel P. Felix

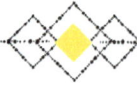

In 2011 he founded the Chicago Trustee Collaboratory, established to articulate, advance, and implement the best practices in trust administration via ongoing peer-to-peer discussions, trainings, and other offerings. Serving as President throughout, Dan oversaw the group's successful acquisition by the Independent Trustee Alliance in 2022.

Dan had cofounded in 2016, and previously served as board member, the Independent Trustee Alliance, the only international professional organization for individual trustees.

Hired to teach lawyers and other professional trust administrators, Dan served as the chair for continuing education of the Illinois State Bar Association's Trust and Estates section from 2020 through 2023. He has written and spoken extensively on trusts and trust administration, including the creation of the Bill of Trust Beneficiary Rights. You can find his articles on his website and in a book collection due out soon.

Dan earned his Bachelor of Arts in American Civilization from the University of Illinois, Urbana and his Juris Doctor from Loyola University of Chicago School of Law. While at Loyola, he served on the Law Journal, won the Loyola ASCAP Copyright Competition, took the helm as President of the International Law Society, and led a team as the managing editor of the *Women's Law Reporter*.

Daniel resides in Illinois with his wife.

Coming Soon!

Trusts
in
SHORT
Articles, Essays, and Other Thoughts on
What's Important in Administering Trusts
Daniel P. Felix